The Death Penalty in America: Current Research

Edited by Robert M. Bohm
University of North Carolina - Charlotte

ACJS Series Editor, Anna Kuhl

Academy of Criminal Justice Sciences
Northern Kentucky University
402 Nunn Hall
Highland Heights, KY 41076

Anderson Publishing Co.
Criminal Justice Division
P.O. Box 1576
Cincinnati, OH 45201-1576

The Death Penalty in America: Current Research

Copyright © 1991 by   Anderson Publishing Co. and
Academy of Criminal Justice Sciences

ISBN 0-87084-013-4

Library of Congress Catalog Number 90-82314

Kelly Humble *Managing Editor*   *Project Editor* Gail Eccleston

Cover Design by John H. Walker

Preface

As Series Editor for the conjoint Monograph Series between the Academy of Criminal Justice Sciences and Anderson Publishing Co., I am excited to introduce the second volume in this series: Robert Bohm's *The Death Penalty in America: Current Research*. This is a book that reviewers have described as on the cutting edge of research specific to the death penalty. Bob has brought together a series of articles by well-known authors who critically examine issues that are specific to the death penalty in America. As Bob so succinctly argues, interest in the death penalty is urgent since there are more than 2,000 persons on death row, which may "portent an imminent return to the rates of executions of the 1930s and the 1940s." What makes this book so exciting is the depth and breadth of the analysis from several points of view, both philosophical and political, by the various authors.

This is the second volume in the Monograph Series, the first being Ralph Weisheit's *Drugs, Crime and the Criminal Justice System*. Soon to follow is Michael Steinman's book on domestic violence, titled *Woman Battering: Policy Responses*. Future volumes include Gary Cordner and Donna Hale's book on "Police Administration." Please keep these volumes in mind either as reference books or as you plan your future classes.

Anna F. Kuhl
Eastern Kentucky University

Acknowledgments

My sincere thanks to the contributors to this volume. Their efforts have made a valuable contribution to the death penalty literature. Thanks also to Hal Pepinsky and Jim Finckenauer for their helpful reviews of the manuscripts and to Dean Thomas Barker and the College of Criminal Justice at Jacksonville State University for their support during the early stages of this endeavor. Finally thanks to Anna Kuhl, ACJS Series Editor, and to Anderson Publishing Company for undertaking the project.

Introduction

With rare exceptions, current research on the death penalty is a peculiarly American enterprise. Furthermore, the American scholars who conduct most of the research are again, with rare exceptions, opponents of the practice. Neither of these two observations should be particularly surprising, since the United States holds the dubious distinction of being the only western industrialized nation to continue to routinely sentence capital offenders to death. Though, currently, "only" 117 people have been executed in the United States since executions resumed in 1977—a relatively small number compared to the 199 people executed in 1935 alone—the more than 2,000 people currently on death row portend an imminent return to the rates of executions of the 1930s and 1940s. Thus, the urgency of the problem, for those who consider it a problem, and not just historical interest, accounts for the growing volume of research on capital punishment in the United States.

Though all of the research contained in this volume was conducted in the last few years, by "current research" I refer to studies conducted after the landmark decision of *Gregg v. Georgia* in 1976. That decision, along with the decisions in two companion cases (*Jurek v. Texas* and *Proffitt v. Florida*), was the constitutional basis for resuming executions in the United States after nearly a decade hiatus. Much of this newer research differs from that which preceded it in two major ways. First, the methodology and statistical analytic techniques used to test hypotheses in the newer research are generally more sophisticated. Second, the issues examined in the newer research are more varied, focusing especially on the administration of the death penalty under post-*Furman* guided discretion statutes. The chapters in this volume exemplify both developments.

Chapter 1, by Victoria Schneider and John Ortiz Smykla, introduces a remarkable new computer-readable data collection of 14,570 legally authorized executions in the United States between 1608 and 1987. Painstakingly documented and confirmed by M. Watt Espy over many years, *The Espy File* contains data on 21 variables and is the most comprehensive collection of information on

American executions available. After critically reviewing various empirical data sources on capital punishment, Schneider and Smykla provide the first descriptive analysis of the Espy data. They provide interesting new insights on historical and regional trends in capital punishment, on the racial, gender, and age characteristics of the condemned, and on the previously ignored subject of slave executions.

Besides faith in the deterrent effect of the death penalty for murder, proponents of capital punishment often assume that the death penalty is a deterrent for crimes that are not capital offenses; that capital punishment is a general prophylactic and a requisite for law and order. Though intuitively appealing to many proponents of capital punishment, until now, the idea that the death penalty serves as a deterrent to crime in general has not been tested empirically. In Chapter 2, William C. Bailey presents the first empirical test of this hypothesis for which he finds no support.

In Chapter 3, Raymond Paternoster addresses an issue that has received a fair amount of recent attention: whether post-*Furman* guided discretion statutes have effectively eliminated the racial discrimination the Court found repugnant under pre-*Furman* statutes. The Court believed that requiring the capital sentencing authority to consider aggravating and mitigating evidence would result in a sentence based only on legally relevant factors. However, left untouched by this procedural reform was a potential source of odious racial bias occurring earlier in the process: the discretion exercised by the prosecutor in deciding whether to seek a death sentence. Paternoster compares the factors that influence prosecutors' charging decisions under the post-*Furman* capital statutes of two contiguous death penalty states, North and South Carolina, and finds strong evidence of victim-based racial discrimination in prosecutorial decision-making in South Carolina but very little in North Carolina.

In Chapter 4, the same theme, the factors that influence a prosecutor's decision to seek the death penalty, is addressed by Thomas J. Keil and Gennaro F. Vito. The authors construct a latent variable, estimated from a tetrachoric correlation matrix, to measure the seriousness of murders in Kentucky. They discover that seriousness is a unidimensional latent variable which consists of both legal and extra-legal factors including race of the offender and race of the victim. They found that the seriousness variable accounts for a little over 40 percent of the variation in Kentucky prosecutors' decisions to seek the death penalty.

Among the vexing issues with the administration of the death penalty are the effects of psychiatric testimony on the sentencing decisions of jurors in capital cases. The issue is important because the future dangerousness of a capital defendant is one of the criteria in many of the post-*Furman* guided discretion death penalty statutes. Psychiatric testimony often is used to make such a prediction. Yet, the Supreme Court determined that psychiatric testimony in the sentencing phase of a capital trial can be prejudicial to the interests of a defendant. In Chapter 5,

Frank P. Williams III and Marilyn D. McShane examine the levels of trust that prospective jurors place in psychologists and psychiatrists and the effects of their testimony alleging defendant mental problems on the decisions of capital jurors. They conclude that psychiatric testimony on the side of the prosecution is ascribed more credibility than psychiatric testimony on the side of the defense. A result is an increase in the conviction rate, especially for death-qualified juries (those juries comprised of people who are not categorically opposed to capital punishment). Prospective death-qualified jurors seem to view temporary insanity as an aggravating, rather than a mitigating, circumstance. The authors also indicate that black defendants are particularly disadvantaged in the conviction phase of a capital trial when psychiatric testimony alleging temporary insanity is used. Regarding sentencing, the authors found that the psychiatric testimony produced fewer death sentences for all defendants. Thus, psychiatric testimony regarding temporary insanity appears to disadvantage capital defendants, especially black defendants, during the conviction phase of a capital trial, and benefits them during the sentencing phase.

Perhaps the most defensible justification for capital punishment is incapacitation. That an executed capital offender can never kill again is an unarguable fact. The principal assumption of the incapacitation rationale is that capital offenders pose an extraordinary threat to other inmates and correctional personnel while in prison and to the general public if they are paroled. Chapters 6 and 7 address this issue. In Chapter 6, Gennaro F. Vito, Pat Koester, and Deborah G. Wilson present the results of a recent national survey of the status of death row inmates who had their sentences commuted as a result of the U.S. Supreme Court's decision in *Furman v. Georgia* (1972). The Court's decision in *Furman* provided a natural experiment, and Vito and his colleagues report on the prison behavior and recidivism, including any additional murders, of this cohort. The authors tentatively concluded that the *Furman* parolees performed better than expected. Of the approximately 40 percent of the 457 *Furman*-commuted inmates granted parole, about 20 percent were reincarcerated. The repeat homicide rate for the *Furman* parolees was 1.6 percent (3/185). They also committed 3 robberies, 1 rape, and 1 kidnapping (for a total violent crime rate of 4.5%). Regarding institutional behavior, of the 272 *Furman*-commuted inmates not granted parole, 25 violent offenses (11% of the total number of institutional violations) were committed following their return to the general prison population.

In Chapter 7, Gennaro F. Vito, Deborah G. Wilson, and Edward J. Latessa continue the investigation of *Furman*-commuted death row inmates by comparing the experiences of two contiguous states, Kentucky and Ohio. The authors compare the case and offender characteristics, attributes of victims, system practices, and parole performance of the *Furman*-commuted inmates in the two states. Both similarities and differences were found. Most importantly, both groups had similar recidivism rates, and none of the paroled inmates in either group committed another murder. However, two members of the Ohio cohort committed subsequent murders while in prison. Together, Chapters 6 and 7 provide a more comprehensive understanding of the risk potential of capital offenders.

Chapter 8, my own chapter in the volume, is about American death penalty opinion. Currently, more Americans favor the death penalty for persons convicted of murder than at any time since the first poll on the subject was conducted in 1936. Described in this chapter are the data contained in the Gallup public opinion polls on the death penalty for murder conducted over the 50-year period, 1936-1986 (with some reference to the 1988 poll). Ten demographic characteristics are analyzed: gender, race, age, politics, education, income or SES, occupation, religion, city size, and region of the country. Among the findings is that, even though a majority of people in all demographic categories examined currently support the death penalty, blacks, females, people under 30, Democrats, college graduates, people in the bottom income or SES category, manual laborers, and Easterners and Southerners support the death penalty less than whites, males, Republicans, high school graduates, people in the top income category, clerical and sales workers, and Westerners and Midwesterners. This chapter concludes with a discussion of the problems with death penalty opinion research generally.

Over a decade ago, a well-respected criminologist boldly asserted that everything that could be written about capital punishment had been written! Despite the obvious hyperbole, there is no question that the subject of capital punishment in the United States has commanded much attention during the last 200 years, and especially during the last decade and a half. Nevertheless, the research in this volume is noteworthy because it either fills critical knowledge gaps or contributes importantly to current debates on unresolved issues.

Contents

1

A Summary Analysis of *Executions In The United States, 1608-1987: The Espy File*

Victoria Schneider*
Inter-University Consortium for Political and Social Research
University of Michigan

John Ortiz Smykla
Department of Criminal Justice
The University of Alabama

INTRODUCTION

The issue of capital punishment poses a dilemma that demands our society's careful attention and requires empirical research. Unfortunately, much of the information available on the death penalty has been fragmentary or incomplete, limited in its coverage, and often unreliable. Over the past 30 years, some empirical work on executions under civil authority has been conducted by social scientists (See for example, Bowers, 1984). These analyses have often focused on racial bias in the use of the death penalty and its deterrent effects on crime; regional differences in the application of the death penalty; and arguments in favor of or against capital punishment. Much more work is needed because findings from various analyses on executions in the United States have a serious impact on our understanding of how the death penalty has been applied. Recently, through a project at The University of Alabama, a new comprehensive computer-readable data collection on the history of capital punishment in the United States has

---

* Authors' names appear in alphabetical order according to the first letter of their surnames. Equal effort was made by both authors in preparing this chapter.

1

become available. The general purpose of this chapter is to provide summary analysis from the 14,570 cases in this collection, *Executions in the United States, 1608-1987* by M. Watt Espy and John Ortiz Smykla.[1]

As mentioned above, to gain more insight on the nature of capital punishment, more empirical work is necessary. It is important that such work be based on information collected over an extended period of time. Previous research extends only to the middle of the nineteenth century to the time of the Civil War. These studies concentrate on executions under civil authority at the state level only (e.g., Teeters & Zibulka, in Bowers, 1984). By covering a longer period of time and including executions at the local level, a more comprehensive view of the various trends in the application of capital punishment, such as frequency of use, racial and gender differences, and regional variations, is possible.

This chapter has two main purposes: First, to describe various empirical data sources on capital punishment concentrating especially on their coverage, strong points, and limitations. Second, to introduce *Executions in the United States, 1608-1987: The Espy File* (hereafter referred to as *The Espy File*); to explain the data collection procedures used to create the file; to describe the variables included in the collection; to highlight the important features of the collection which overcome various limitations in other data sources; to provide summary analysis; and to compare our findings on historical trends in executions to those of other social scientists.

DATA SOURCES ON EXECUTIONS IN THE UNITED STATES

There are six major data sources on executions in the United States. The first is known as the Teeters-Zibulka inventory. It contains information on executions from January 20, 1864 to August 10, 1967 obtained from Department of Corrections' officials or agencies in each state. The inventory lists the name, age at execution, race, offense, state, county, method of execution, and presence of appeal for 5,706 cases. All executions in the file were carried out under state authority, specifically under the auspices of a state penal institution (Teeters & Zibulka in Bowers, 1984).

The Teeters-Zibulka inventory is limited to only executions performed after authority was centralized at the state level and record-keeping was routinized, and does not contain any local authority executions. The first state to centralize authority was Vermont in 1864 and Louisiana was the last in 1957. Delaware and Montana have never removed execution authority from the local level (Bowers, 1984).

A second major data source on executions in the United States is the official government collection first published by the Census Bureau and the Federal Bureau of Prisons and now published by the Bureau of Justice Statistics. Beginning in 1850, the federal government began reporting mortality figures from executions in the population census reports (United States Department of Interior, Bureau of the Census, 1854 and 1864). Then in 1880 national government statistics on capital punishment were reported in a special publication produced by the Census Bureau called *Dependent, Defective, and Delinquent* (United States Department of Interior, Bureau of the Census, 1888). Other publications were issued in 1904, and in 10-year intervals until 1930, at which time the Census Bureau series, *Prisoners in State and Federal Reformations,* began to contain a special section on executions (United States Department of Commerce, Bureau of the Census 1929).[2] This series was transferred to the Bureau of Prisons in 1947; to the Law Enforcement Assistance Administration (LEAA) in 1971; and finally, since 1978, has been published by the U.S. Department of Justice, Bureau of Justice Statistics (BJS) (Cahalan & Parsons, 1986). Annually, BJS provides detailed information on prisoners under death sentences from data collected by the National Prisoner Statistics (NPS) program. In its 1987 summary, BJS reported 3,952 executions under civil authority since 1930 (United States Department of Justice, Bureau of Justice Statistics, 1988). This figure includes 3,919 executions under state authority and 33 under federal jurisdiction. It does not include any executions under local authority.

Bowers (1984) compared the Teeters-Zibulka inventory to the first longitudinal collection produced by the National Prisoner Statistics (NPS) program (United States Department of Justice, Bureau of Prisons, 1971). The Teeters-Zibulka inventory reported 3,567 executions from 1930 to 1967, while the NPS collection, for the same years, reported 3,859 under all civil authority, both state and local auspices (although no distinction between the two is made). The difference in the number of executions between the two collections is 292, and according to Bowers this reflects the fact that five states, Louisiana, Missouri, Montana, Delaware, and Mississippi continued to conduct local executions after 1930. Regarding offenses leading to executions, Bowers found the two data sources almost identical. The Teeters-Zibulka data showed slightly more (0.1%) executions for murder and slightly fewer (0.1%) executions for rape than the NPS data. Some difference in the race of offender was also found. The NPS data reported that 54.6 percent of those executed were nonwhites, while the Teeters-Zibulka collection found 58.5 percent. Bowers notes that this difference is due to missing data on race in the Teeters-Zibulka listing.

Jurisdiction over execution reveals further differences between NPS data and the Teeters-Zibulka inventory. The NPS data contain information on locally imposed executions that were excluded from the Teeters-Zibulka listing. And the Teeters-Zibulka inventory has data on federal executions performed at state facilities that are not included in the NPS data. Overall, Bowers concludes that the Teeters-Zibulka listing is a complete inventory of state-imposed executions since 1930 (Bowers, 1984).

The next four data collections extend over a much shorter period of time than the Teeters-Zibulka inventory or the NPS series. The *Chicago Tribune* reported that between 1901 and 1917 a total of 1,858 legal executions were performed. In addition, the *Tribune* estimated that, from 1896 through 1900, 610 executions occurred. Bye (1919), using the *Tribune* data, reports annual averages of executions for seven time segments between 1890 and 1917:

(1) 1890 to 1895—121 per year;   (5) 1911 to 1915—99 per year;
(2) 1896 to 1900—122 per year;   (6) 916—117 per year;
(3) 1901 to 1905—126 per year;   (7) 1917—85 per year.
(4) 1906 to 1910—106 per year;

Barnes and Teeters (1943) report that there were 564 executions from 1925 through 1929. Although they give no source for their data, they report that 123 executions occurred in 1925, 104 in 1926, 118 in 1927, 132 in 1928, and 87 in 1929 for an average of 112.8 per year. Bedau (1982) says these figures should be corrected upward reflecting later work done by Sellin. Using data from the Illinois Department of Welfare, Sellin (1950) reported the total for this period as 591: for 1927, 139 executions; for 1928, 135; and for 1929, 90 lawful executions.

Prior to the production of *The Espy File,* Bedau (1982) declared that no known figures on annual executions in the United States existed for the years 1918 to 1924. He estimated 114 per year across these six years by averaging the number of executions for selected periods of time before and after this interval. He chose the mid-point between the annual average for 1901 to 1917, or 109.3 executions, and the annual average for 1925 to 1929, or 118.2 executions. The resulting average for 1921 to 1924 was 114 executions.

EXECUTIONS IN THE UNITED STATES, 1608-1987: THE ESPY FILE

Methodology

The data for this project were originally collected by M. Watt Espy beginning in 1970 using his own resources. Later his work was supported by The University of Alabama Law Center and the National Science Foundation.[3] Through July 6, 1987, Espy confirmed 14,570 executions performed in the United States under civil authority starting with the execution of Captain George Kendall in 1608. *The Espy File* does not include executions imposed since July 6, 1987 or any other executions confirmed by Espy after the close of this project.

For many years Espy collected and recorded information about executions throughout the United States on two ledgers. One contained executions by state in chronological order and had information, as available, on the name, age, race, occupation of offender, place and jurisdiction of execution, crime, county of conviction, date and method of execution, and if the case was a slave execution, whether or not the owner or executioner was compensated. The second ledger had a listing of the same cases in chronological order only. Data recorded in both ledgers were assigned numeric codes and organized into a format so that a single execution became a case in a computer-readable data file (Espy & Smykla, 1987).

Espy used a variety of data collection procedures in his efforts to obtain a complete listing of all executions performed in the United States under civil authority. For persons executed under state authority, he consulted State Departments of Corrections. In the process of collecting and confirming executions, he independently validated (and corrected or added data when necessary) all executions in the Teeters-Zibulka inventory by conducting an exhaustive search of other official sources. These sources were contemporary newspaper accounts in their original form, microfilmed records, and secondary records including direct and indirect historical information. When several sources were employed to confirm an execution, they were compared for completeness.

When data sources reported conflicting items about a particular execution, such as differences in the date of an execution or the offender's age, special decision rules were adopted. The most authoritative sources were always appeals court records and state and regional official legal records. In most cases appeals court records were not published prior to the early nineteenth century, and even then capital cases were only appealed based on the offender's resources. For executions occurring prior to the early nineteenth century, newspapers from the state or city where they took place were accepted as authoritative sources over ones from other cities, counties, or states.

As stated above, the data were made computer-readable from information taken directly from the two ledgers created by Espy. The computer-readable version was checked for errors by comparisons made with the original ledgers, the coding sheets, and the typed verbatim transcriptions of information from the various sources. In addition, Espy confirmed each piece of information in the public use file (Espy & Smykla, 1987).

As noted, *The Espy File* contains 21 variables, including the name, race, age, and occupation of the offender, county of conviction, place and jurisdiction of execution, crime, date and method of execution, and, if the case was a slave execution, whether or not the owner or executioner was compensated. In the pages that follow trends in *The Espy File* are highlighted and comparisons with Bowers' (1984) data are made.

Historical and Regional Developments

Table 1.1 presents a summary of all state and local executions conducted under civil authority included in *The Espy File*. To present the data across four centuries, we provide totals and percentages for all state and local executions conducted under civil authority in the seventeenth and eighteenth centuries.

Because of the influence of the Civil War on nineteenth-century politics we provide execution totals through 1865. Thereafter we adopt Bowers' use of decades so that we might offer some comparisons.

Table 1.1 Summary of *Executions in the United States, 1608-1987: The Espy File*

Years	Total Local and State Executions	Percentage	Developmental Period
1600s	162	1.11	
1700s	1391	9.56	Growth Period
1800-1865	2453	16.86	
1866-1879	825	5.67	
1880s	1005	6.91	
1890s	1098	7.55	
1900s	1280	8.80	Period of Stability
1910s	1091	7.50	
1920s	1289	8.86	
1930s	1676	11.52	Peak Period
1940s	1284	8.83	
1950s	715	4.91	Period of Decline
1960-1987	272	1.87	
Total	14541*	99.95	

*The total number of cases in *The Espy File* is 14,570. The total here is less due to cases where place of execution was unknown and under "other authority."

The data in Table 1.1 show that one-third (or 4,831) of the total number of local and state executions in *The Espy File* occurred before 1880. We label this period one of *growth* because the number of executions progressively increased since the first confirmed execution of George Kendall in Virginia in 1608. By comparison, only one-half of one percent of the executions recorded by Bowers occurred before 1880, a period he labels dormancy (Bowers, 1984:50). The differences between the two data sets for this time period [at this level] alone demonstrate the historical significance of *The Espy File*.

The data in Table 1.1 also show that for the next five decades (1880-1920) the number of state and local executions in the United States *stabilized*, averaging 1,148 per decade. The number of state and local executions in Bowers (1984: 53-54) begins with 1890 and produces a similar average (1,153) across four begins with 1890 and produces a similar average (1,153) across four decades, (1890-1920) using *estimates* (emphasis in the original) and some data with no sources. Comparing the Bowers and Espy data across these four decades we find that Espy confirmed 143 (or 3%) more state and local executions.

The *peak* execution period for any one decade is the 1930s. *The Espy File* confirms 1,676 executions (1,463 under state-authority and 213 under local-authority) during the 1930s. Bowers too characterizes the 1930s as the *peak* decade in executions since 1880 (Bowers, 1984:50). Bowers, however, recorded 1,523 state-authority and 147 local-authority executions (54). In short, *The Espy File* confirms a total of six more executions than Bowers for the decade of the 1930s. Espy confirmed 60 fewer state-authority executions but 66 more local-authority executions than Bowers.

Another measure of the importance of *The Espy File* can be seen in Table 1.2. Here the number of executions conducted under state and local authority are compared with those given in Bowers (1984:54). An examination of Table 1.2 shows that Espy documents civil executions conducted under local authority dating back to the 1600s. None are included in Bowers before 1890. Those that Bowers includes for the decades prior to the 1930s are *estimates* (emphasis in the original, 53) and the number of local executions for the period 1921 to 1926 carry no sources in the original (53). *The Espy File* confirms 5,788 civil executions conducted under local authority from 1608 through 1889. This represents about 66 percent of all civil executions conducted under local authority and approximately 40 percent of all executions in *The Espy File*, an important historical contribution.

Table 1.2 Comparison of Legally Imposed Executions Conducted Under Local and State Authority in Espy and Bowers

| | Espy | | Bowers | |
| | Local Authority | State Authority | Local Authority | State Authority |
Years				
1600s	162	0	(None given	(None given
1700s	1391	0	before	before
1800-1865	2441	10	1890)	1853)
1866-1879	805	15		33**
1880s	989	16		30
1890s	949	149	1060	155
1900s	997	283	901	291
1910s	397	694	406	633
1920s	274	1015	131	1038
1930s	213	1463	147	1523
1940s	143	1141	110	1178
1950s	45	670	35	681
1960 and later*	2	189	0	191

The Espy File includes executions through July 6, 1987. Bowers' data are provided through December, 1982.

**These data are presented in Bowers as 1870 and earlier.

A close inspection of Table 1.2 also reveals that the coverage and completeness of the data collected on state and local executions by one investigator (Espy) have produced results different than data collected by multiple investigators, each using different techniques, as reported in Bowers (1984). *The Espy File* documents 118 fewer executions under state authority since 1866 than the estimated and uncited sources in Bowers (50). Also, *The Espy File* documents 230 more local authority executions than the collected sources presented in Bowers (53, 54) since 1890.

With *The Espy File* we can also reexamine historical trends in capital punishment by region. One obvious limitation in Bowers' description of developmental patterns in capital punishment is that it relies only on civil executions conducted under state authority. *The Espy File,* by including data on both state and local executions, changes some of Bowers' interpretations.

Figure 1.1 graphically depicts trends in the use of combined state and local authority executions for the North, the South, and the West of the United States. Whereas Bowers (1984:51-52) concludes on the basis of state authority executions from 1880 through the 1920s that more executions were imposed in the North than in any other region of the United States, *The Espy File* documents that more executions imposed under civil authority were conducted in the South than in the North or West.

The addition of local authority executions also corrects Bowers' (1984:51) conclusion that the rise and fall in legally imposed executions were most pronounced in the South. The data accompanying Figure 1.1 reveal that the average percentage change in legally imposed executions since the nineteenth century is greater in the North (an average of negative 14.2%) than in the South (an average of negative 8.45%).

Our discussion of regional differences also focuses on the number of executions for murder, rape, and combinations of murder and rape offenses. Table 1.3 shows the number of executions for murder, rape, and combinations of murder and rape offenses by region and time. Unfortunately, too few executions for rape outside the South (57) precluded comparison across time and region for this offense.

The addition of local-authority executions refines our knowledge of the historical patterns of executions in the United States begun by Bowers (1984:49-58). We find in Table 1.3 that the pattern for executions for murder in the South and in the rest of the country are not as comparable as Bowers (57) suggests. Executions for murder peaked in the North in the 1920s and in the South in the 1930s. However, executions for murder in the South were almost as high in the 1880s, 1890s, and 1900s as they were in the peak decade of the 1930s.

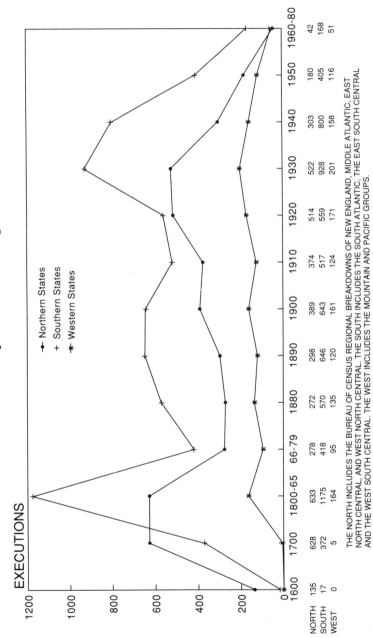

Figure 1.1 State and Local Authority
Executions by Time and Region

THE NORTH INCLUDES THE BUREAU OF CENSUS REGIONAL BREAKDOWNS OF NEW ENGLAND, MIDDLE ATLANTIC, EAST NORTH CENTRAL, AND WEST NORTH CENTRAL. THE SOUTH INCLUDES THE SOUTH ATLANTIC, THE EAST SOUTH CENTRAL AND THE WEST SOUTH CENTRAL. THE WEST INCLUDES THE MOUNTAIN AND PACIFIC GROUPS.

Table 1.3 Executions by Region[a] and Type of Offense, 1600s to 1987

Years	Murder	Rape	Combination[b]	Murder	Rape	Combination	Murder	Rape	Combination
		North			South			West	
1600s	40	7	5	9	0	1	0	0	0
1700s	175	19	24	118	5	10	1	0	0
1800-1865	425	8	143	567	39	94	118	0	23
1866-1879	155	1	99	284	36	77	79	0	14
1880s	201	1	64	442	35	75	111	0	22
1890s	218	2	75	467	45	123	89	0	25
1900s	278	2	107	456	75	103	23	0	36
1910s	275	6	85	359	57	93	88	0	36
1920s	307	0	201	330	75	150	131	0	39
1930s	279	4	235	484	112	311	125	0	73
1940s	153	3	137	383	172	226	86	0	68
1950s	82	1	94	191	84	124	54	0	61
1960s-1980s	17	3	21	62	23	79	24	0	4
Totals	2605	57	1290	4152	758	1466	929	0	401

[a] The North includes the Bureau of Census regional breakdowns of New England, Middle Atlantic, East North Central, and West North Central. The South includes the South Atlantic, the East South Central, and the West South Central. The West includes the Mountain and Pacific groups.

[b] The combination offenses include rape/murder, robbery/murder, accessory to murder, murder/rape/robbery, burglary/attempted rape, attempted rape, murder/burglary, kidnap/murder, kidnap/murder/robbery, arson/murder, rape/robbery, and attempted murder.

Our analysis is also able to correct Bowers' (1984:57) finding that during the 1890s, 1910s, and 1920s the South lagged behind the rest of the country by about 200 executions per decade for murder. Comparing data from *The Epsy File* with Bowers' data by decade beginning with 1880 we find only two decades when the South executed fewer persons for murder than the North and West combined. First, in the 1910s the South executed four fewer persons than the North and West combined (359 and 363, respectively) and then again in the 1920s the South executed 330 persons for murder compared to 438 in the North and West. In all other decades since 1880 the South has executed more persons for murder than the North and West combined. Furthermore, we found that the average number of executions for murder in the South per decade during the 1930s, 1940s, and 1950s was 93, not 50 as reported by Bowers. Finally, it is instructive to note that since 1800, executions for murder in the South have exceeded executions for murder in the North or West (taken separately) by substantial margins.

Characteristics of the Condemned

This section of our analysis reports on the extent to which historical and regional trends were accompanied by changes in the characteristics of the condemned. The characteristics discussed here are race, gender, age, and slave status.

Race

Tables 1.4, 1.5, and 1.6 compare the number and percentage of white, black, and other races executed under state and local authority in the South and North and West (the latter two combined) since the 1600s for the offenses of murder, rape, and combinations of murder/rape offenses. This format of presenting the data was chosen to allow some comparisons with Bowers' (1984:59) data. *The Espy File*, however, offers raw data and data for more crimes on more racial groups across more time periods. Bowers' analysis is limited to raw data and percentages for two crimes (murder and rape) for nonwhites since 1890.

Table 1.4 Number and Percentage of Whites Executed Under State and Local Authority Per Decade by Offense and Region[a]

Years	Murder		Rape		Combination[b]	
	North/West	South	North/West	South	North/West	South
1600s	20 (55.55)	6 (66.66)	2 (28.57)	0	5 (100.00)	0
1700s	94 (64.38)	46 (42.59)	4 (25.00)	0	19 (82.60)	7 (70.00)
1800-1865	360 (72.72)	228 (41.68)	13 (76.47)	0	111 (67.68)	35 (38.46)
1866-1879	160 (76.92)	55 (22.08)	0	0	83 (77.57)	22 (30.13)
1880s	217 (75.87)	77 (18.33)	0	2 (5.71)	68 (82.92)	19 (26.38)
1890s	183 (68.53)	84 (18.96)	0	2 (4.65)	68 (74.72)	38 (32.47)
1900s	251 (67.47)	79 (17.91)	0	5 (6.75)	102 (73.38)	17 (17.00)
1910s	235 (66.76)	81 (23.54)	0	5 (8.77)	94 (81.03)	15 (16.12)
1920s	270 (63.67)	108 (33.23)	0	9 (12.00)	172 (72.57)	56 (37.33)
1930s	279 (72.65)	145 (30.39)	0	6 (5.35)	233 (76.64)	99 (31.83)
1940s	139 (60.96)	103 (27.39)	0	19 (11.11)	115 (59.27)	56 (24.77)
1950s	84 (66.14)	79 (42.02)	0	13 (15.47)	93 (62.41)	36 (29.03)
1960s-1980s	24 (60.00)	34 (54.83)	0	4 (17.39)	28 (63.63)	32 (40.50)
Totals	2316 (68.82)	1125 (28.20)	19 (33.33)	65 (8.65)	1191 (71.96)	432 (29.87)

[a]The North includes the Bureau of Census regional breakdowns of New England, Middle Atlantic, East North Central, and West North Central. The South includes the South Atlantic, the East South Central, and the West South Central. The West includes the Mountain and Pacific groups.

[b]The combination offenses include rape/murder, robbery/murder, accessory to murder, murder/rape/robbery, burglary/attempted rape, attempted rape, murder/burglary, kidnap/murder, kidnap/murder/robbery, arson/murder, rape/robbery, and attempted murder.

Table 1.5 Number and Percentage of Blacks Executed Under State and Local Authority Per Decade by Offense and Region[a]

Years	Murder		Rape		Combination[b]	
	North/West	South	North/West	South	North/West	South
1600s	7 (19.44)	2 (22.22)	4 (57.14)	0	0	0
1700s	32 (21.91)	59 (54.62)	12 (75.00)	5 (100.00)	4 (17.39)	3 (30.00)
1800-1865	60 (12.12)	284 (51.91)	4 (23.52)	38 (100.00)	12 (7.31)	55 (60.43)
1866-1879	18 (8.65)	170 (68.27)	1 (100.00)	34 (100.00)	14 (13.08)	43 (58.90)
1880s	34 (11.88)	311 (74.04)	1 (100.00)	33 (94.28)	9 (10.97)	47 (65.27)
1890s	53 (19.85)	331 (74.71)	2 (100.00)	40 (93.02)	17 (18.68)	76 (64.95)
1900s	77 (20.69)	354 (80.27)	1 (50.00)	66 (89.18)	32 (23.02)	83 (83.00)
1910s	68 (19.31)	256 (74.41)	6 (100.00)	52 (91.22)	18 (15.51)	76 (81.72)
1920s	102 (24.05)	214 (65.84)	0	66 (88.00)	53 (22.36)	90 (60.00)
1930s	68 (17.70)	320 (67.08)	2 (100.00)	104 (92.85)	62 (20.39)	208 (66.88)
1940s	70 (30.70)	269 (71.54)	2 (100.00)	150 (87.71)	74 (38.14)	165 (73.00)
1950s	34 (26.77)	108 (57.44)	1 (100.00)	71 (84.52)	41 (27.51)	88 (70.96)
1960s-1980s	11 (27.50)	25 (40.32)	0	19 (82.60)	13 (29.54)	43 (54.43)
Totals	634 (18.84)	2703 (67.76)	36 (63.15)	678 (90.27)	349 (21.08)	977 (67.56)

[a]The North includes the Bureau of Census regional breakdowns of New England, Middle Atlantic, East North Central, and West North Central. The South includes the South Atlantic, the East South Central, and the West South Central. The West includes the Mountain and Pacific groups.

[b]The combination offenses include rape/murder, robbery/murder, accessory to murder, murder/rape/robbery, burglary/attempted rape, attempted rape, murder/burglary, kidnap/murder, kidnap/murder/robbery, arson/murder, rape/robbery, and attempted murder.

Table 1.6 Number and Percentage of Other Races[a] Executed Under State and Local Authority Per Decade by Offense and Region[b]

Years	Murder		Rape		Combination[b]	
	North/West	South	North/West	South	North/West	South
1600s	9 (25.00)	1 (11.11)	1 (14.28)	0	0	0
1700s	20 (13.69)	3 (2.77)	0	0	0	0
1800-1865	75 (15.15)	35 (6.39)	0	0	41 (25.00)	1 (1.09)
1866-1879	30 (14.42)	24 (9.63)	0	0	10 (9.34)	8 (10.95)
1880s	35 (12.23)	32 (7.61)	0	0	5 (6.09)	6 (8.33)
1890s	31 (11.61)	28 (6.32)	0	1 (2.32)	6 (6.59)	3 (2.56)
1900s	44 (11.82)	8 (1.81)	1 (50.00)	3 (4.05)	5 (3.59)	0
1910s	49 (13.92)	7 (2.03)	0	0	4 (3.44)	2 (2.15)
1920s	52 (12.26)	3 (0.92)	0	0	12 (5.06)	4 (2.66)
1930s	37 (9.63)	12 (2.51)	0	2 (1.78)	9 (2.96)	4 (1.28)
1940s	19 (8.33)	4 (1.06)	0	2 (1.16)	5 (2.57)	5 (2.21)
1950s	9 (7.08)	1 (0.53)	0	0	15 (10.06)	0
1960s-1980s	5 (12.50)	3 (4.83)	0	0	3 (6.81)	4 (5.06)
Totals	415 (12.33)	161 (4.03)	2 (3.50)	8 (1.06)	115 (6.94)	37 (2.55)

[a]Other races include Native American (353), Asian or Pacific Islander (142), Hispanic (301), and Other (2).

[b]The North includes the Bureau of Census regional breakdowns of New England, Middle Atlantic, East North Central, and West North Central. The South includes the South Atlantic, the East South Central, and the West South Central. The West includes the Mountain and Pacific groups.

[c]The combination offenses include rape/murder, robbery/murder, accessory to murder, murder/rape/robbery, burglary/attempted rape, attempted rape, murder/burglary, kidnap/murder, kidnap/murder/robbery, arson/murder, rape/robbery, and attempted murder.

Concerning the race of persons executed in the United States under state and local authority, the data in Tables 1.4, 1.5, and 1.6 reveal substantial variation by region and offense. Bowers reports similar conclusions. Unlike Bowers, however, we find moderate variation within categories over time.

For murder in the North and West, approximately 69 percent of those executed were white, 19 percent were black, and 12 percent were other races. Since 1880, variation within these categories across time for the North and West ranges from approximately 76 percent in the 1880s for whites to 60 percent in the 1960s and later; 12 percent in the 1880s for blacks to 31 percent in the 1940s; and 14 percent in the 1910s for other races to 7 percent in the 1950s.

For murder in the South, approximately 28 percent of those executed were white, 68 percent were black, and 4 percent were other races. Since 1880 there has been considerable variation for both whites and blacks. The percent of whites executed for murder in the South ranges from a low of about 18 percent in the 1900s to a high of about 55 percent in the 1960s and later. For blacks, the spread in the range is similar but the values are reversed: from a high of about 80 percent in the 1900s to a low of about 40 percent in the 1960s and later.

Tables 1.4, 1.5, and 1.6 show that since 1880, executions for rape were (with one exception) reserved for blacks in the South. For rape in the South, nine out of ten executions were imposed on blacks in each decade throughout the history of capital punishment until the 1940s and later, when the figure drops a few points below the 90 percent mark.

Regarding executions in the North and West for combinations of murder or rape, Tables 1.4, 1.5, and 1.6 show that approximately 72 percent were white, 21 percent were black, and 7 percent were other races. Since 1880, there is less variation within this category than there is for murder alone.

Execution of combination murder-rape offenses in the South was about 30 percent for whites, 68 percent for blacks, and 3 percent for other races. Relatively little variation within these categories is found since 1880.

In sum, we concur with Bowers (1984:60) that the racial composition of those executed for specific crimes inside and outside the South has remained remarkably steady across the twentieth century. However, we did find that as the proportion of whites executed for murder in the South steadily increased from about 18 percent in the 1880s to about 55 percent in the 1960s and later, the proportion of blacks executed for murder in the South steadily decreased from approximately 80 percent in the 1900s to about 40 percent in the 1960s and later. Quite possibly these data reflect changes in population migration, criminal procedure, and attitudes toward punishment.

Gender

Table 1.7 presents data from *The Espy File* on gender and jurisdiction of those executed. The first woman executed was Jane Champion (age unknown) in

James City County, Virginia, in 1632. Champion was hanged for an unknown crime. The last woman executed was Velma Barfield, age 52, in Robeson County, North Carolina, on November 2, 1984. Barfield was executed by lethal injection for murder.

Women represent two and one-half percent of all persons executed under state and local authority since 1608. Ninety percent of women executed were executed under local authority and the majority (87%) were executed under local authority prior to 1866.

Table 1.7 Historical Trends by Sex and Jurisdiction of Those Executed

Years	Both State & Local		Local Only		State Only	
	Male	Female	Male	Female	Male	Female
1600s	120	42	120	42	—	—
1700s	1249	100	1249	100	—	—
1800-1865	2205	139	2193	139	10	0
1866-1879	814	11	794	11	15	0
1880s	991	13	976	12	15	1
1890s	1086	12	938	11	148	1
1900s	1277	3	996	1	281	2
1910s	1094	1	397	0	693	1
1920s	1286	3	372	2	1014	1
1930s	1668	11	210	3	1455	8
1940s	1284	12	141	2	1131	10
1950s	716	8	45	0	662	8
1960s-1980s	271	2	10	0	260	2
Totals	14061	357	8441	323	5684	34

Age

Data on mean age at execution among those executed under state and local authority per decade by offense and region are presented in Table 1.8. Espy's addition of executions under local authority does not substantially change Bowers' conclusion that the pattern of mean age is equally uniform over time and that most of the variability occurs by offense and region of the country (1984:60). As shown in Table 1.8, mean age at execution was highest for murderers in the North and West, next highest for murderers in the South, followed by persons executed for combination offenses of murder or rape, and lowest for rapists in the South. Across time and place rape generally has been committed by younger offenders than has murder.

The mean age for murderers in the South was 31.5 years and 33.7 years for murderers in the North and West. The mean age for rapists in the South was 25.9 years and 27.6 years for combination offenses in the South. The youngest person (non-slave) executed in the United States was Ocuish Hannah, age 12, in New London County, Connecticut, on December 20, 1786. Hannah was hanged for murder. The oldest person executed was Joe Lee, age 83, in Caroline County, Virginia, on April 21, 1916. Lee was electrocuted for murder.

Table 1.8 Mean Age at Execution Among Those Executed Under State and Local Authority Per Decade by Offense and Region[a]

Years	Murder		Rape	Combination[b]
	South	North/West	South	South
1800-1865	29.2(44)	31.6(29)	—	31.1(12)
1869-1879	28.1(61)	31.8(82)	23.8(12)	28.2(23)
1880s	29.3(124)	34.4(130)	26.2(12)	25.1(24)
1890s	27.8(119)	35.1(141)	24.8(19)	26.3(47)
1900s	30.9(103)	32.4(219)	26.0(21)	25.7(23)
1910s	31.9(108)	33.0(255)	23.7(20)	28.4(25)
1920s	33.2(152)	33.4(327)	26.2(39)	26.5(86)
1930s	31.8(355)	33.3(366)	28.4(92)	27.5(250)
1940s	32.3(263)	33.9(219)	26.2(140)	26.2(197)
1950s	38.1(160)	37.3(131)	27.1(66)	28.8(110)
1960s-1980s	34.2(23)	34.8(40)	27.3(15)	29.9(77)
All years	31.5(1512)	33.7(1939)	25.9(436)	27.6(874)

[a]The North includes the Bureau of Census regional breakdowns of New England, Middle Atlantic, East North Central, and West North Central. The South includes the South Atlantic, the East South Central, and the West South Central. The West includes the Mountain and Pacific groups.

[b]The combination offenses include rape/murder, robbery/murder, accessory to murder, murder/rape/robbery, burglary/attempted rape, attempted rape, murder/burglary, kidnap/murder, kidnap/murder/robbery, arson/murder, rape/robbery, and attempted murder.

Table 1.8 also reveals some interesting fluctuations in age at execution. Mean age at execution peaks in the 1950s for murderers both inside (38.1 years) and outside (37.3 years) the South, peaks in the 1930s for rapists (28.4 years), and peaks in the early nineteenth century for persons executed for combination murder/rape offenses (31.1 years). Bowers (1984:61) reports similar peak periods, although lower ages (34.8, 33.2, and 28.3 years for murderers both inside and outside the South and rapists, respectively). Bowers does not include data on age at execution for combination murder/rape offenses.

The data in Table 1.8 also show that persons executed for murder in the South in the twentieth century were older than persons executed for murder in the South in the nineteenth century. The mean age for murderers in the North and West, however, did not change substantially across both centuries (with the exception of the 1950s). These data conflict with Bowers' conclusion that age at execution for murder drops across the twentieth century (1984:60), save the peaks of the 1950s.

Slave Status

Data on slave executions are a unique feature of *The Espy File*. Table 1.9 summarizes some of the data. A total of 1,749 slave executions are recorded in the file. Almost 83 percent of the slaves executed are male. Nine out of every ten slaves executed were executed in the South. None were executed in the West. Almost two-thirds were executed in the first six and one-half decades of the nineteenth century. Slaves executed for murder or revolt represent one-half of all slave executions.

Table 1.9 Characteristics of Slave Executions

Number of slave executions		1,749	
Gender:	males	1,447	(82.73%)
	females	154	(8.81%)
	missing	148	(8.46%)
Region:	North	145	(8.35%)
	South	1,604	(91.65%)
Year:	1600-1699	17	(0.97%)
	1700-1799	617	(35.27%)
	1800-1865	1,115	(63.75%)
Offenses:	murder	657	(37.56%)
	slave revolt	266	(15.20%)
	rape	113	(6.46%)
	unspecified felony	96	(5.48%)
	housebreaking/burglary	88	(5.03%)
	arson	68	(3.88%)
	poisoning	58	(3.31%)
	attempted murder	50	(2.85%)
	attempted rape	25	(1.42%)
	robbery	19	(1.08%)
	theft/stealing	11	(0.62%)
	robbery/murder	8	(0.45%)
	horse stealing	7	(0.40%)
	rape/murder	6	(0.34%)
	burglary/attempted rape	5	(0.28%)
	conspiracy to commit murder	4	(0.22%)
	arson/rape/murder	3	(0.17%)
	other	3	(0.17%)
	witchcraft	1	(0.05%)
	desertion	1	(0.05%)
	murder/burglary	1	(0.05%)
	sodomy/buggery/bestiality	1	(0.05%)
	aiding runaway slaves	1	(0.05%)
	unknown	257	(14.69%)

The first male slave executed was Jan Creoli (age unknown) in 1651 in New York County, New York for the offense of sodomy/buggery/bestiality. The method of execution is unknown. The last male slave executed was March (Gleason). (The slave was known only as March and Gleason is the owner's surname.) March (age unknown) was hanged in Mobile County, Alabama, on January 6, 1865, for an unknown crime. Two boys, age 12, were the youngest male slaves ever executed. Bill (James) was hanged in Woodford County, Kentucky, on July 30, 1791 for murder. Clem (Seat) was hanged in Sussex County, Virginia, on May 11, 1787, for murder. The oldest male slave executed was Mirilton (Lebreton), age 45, in Orleans County, Louisiana, on June 20, 1771. Mirilton was hanged for murder.

The first female slave executed was Marja (Lamb), age unknown, in Suffolk County, Massachusetts, on September 22, 1681. Marja was burned for arson. The last (and also the youngest) female slave executed was Amy Spain, age 17, in Darlington County, South Carolina, on March 10, 1865. Spain was hanged for an unknown crime. The oldest female slave executed was 65. Her first name is not known but her owner's surname was Green. She was hanged in Prince William County, Virginia, on February 13, 1857, for murder.

CONCLUSION

The primary purpose of this chapter was to introduce the data file, *Executions in the United States, 1608-1987: The Epsy File,* through summary analyses and direct comparisons with the data provided by Bowers (1984). Overall, we found that one major advantage of *The Epsy File* is that it contains data on local-level executions. This addition, in turn, allows for a more comprehensive picture of the nature of executions in the seventeenth, eighteenth, and nineteenth centuries. Previous collections only included information on state executions, of which most occurred during the twentieth century.

We found significant differences between *The Epsy File* and Bowers' (1984) findings with regard to regional variations in executions over time. Our analysis by offense found that the pattern of executions for murder in the South and in the rest of the country are not as comparable as Bowers originally suggested. Since the 1880s, the number of executions in the Southern states has always exceeded the number of executions in other regions.

This chapter also provides breakdowns on the characteristics of those executed. Concerning the race of persons executed, we found substantial variation by region and offense. Capital punishment has been predominantly imposed on whites in the North and West and on blacks in the South, regardless of offense. However, we found some variation in these data. For example, as the proportion of whites executed for murder in the South steadily increased across the twentieth century, the proportion of blacks executed for murder in the South steadily decreased. We also found that execution for rape historically has been imposed on blacks regardless of region. Such distinctions allow for further analysis on racial discrimination patterns in capital punishment over time and according to region.

Our analysis of gender found that only 357 women have been executed under state or local authority since 1608, the majority (79%) before 1866.

The findings on age indicate that the pattern of mean age at execution is uniform over time with variability by offense and region. Mean age at execution was highest for murderers in the North and West (33.7 years) and lowest for rapists in the South (25.9 years).

And finally we also introduced selected characteristics of slave executions in America, a unique feature of *The Espy File*. Documented are 1,749 slave executions, the majority occurring between 1800-1865 for murder or slave revolt.

We hope the data presented in this chapter and in *The Espy File* provide researchers greater insight into the historical practice of capital punishment in the United States.

NOTES

[1]   The data and tabulations utilized in this chapter were made available by the Interuniversity Consortium for Political and Social Research. The data for *Executions in the United States, 1608-1987: The Espy File* were originally collected and prepared by M. Watt Espy and John Ortiz Smykla. The Consortium does not bear any responsibility for the analyses or interpretations presented here. The full citation for the computer-readable data file is: M. Watt Espy and John Ortiz Smykla, *Executions in the United States, 1608-1987: The Espy File* [computer-readable data file] (Tuscaloosa, Ala.: John Ortiz Smykla [producer], 1987); Ann Arbor, Mich.: Interuniversity Consortium for Political and Social Research [distributor], 1987.

[2]   This series continued through 1946.

[3]   The creation of the computer-readable data file was supported by grant #SES-8409725 awarded to The University of Alabama by the National Science Foundation. A sub-grant between The University of Alabama and the University of Michigan provided further work on the data file.

REFERENCES

Barnes, H.E. & N.K. Teeters (1943). *New Horizons in Criminology*. Englewood Cliffs, NJ: Prentice-Hall.

Bedau, H.A. (ed.) (1982). *The Death Penalty in America,* Third Edition. New York: Oxford University Press.

Bowers, W.J. (1984). *Legal Homicide: Death as Punishment in America, 1864-1982.* Boston: Northeastern University Press.

Bye, R.T. (1919). *Capital Punishment in the United States.* Philadelphia: The Committee of Philanthropic Labor of Friends.

Cahalan, M.W. & L.L. Parsons (1986). *Historical Corrections Statistics in the United States, 1850-1984.* Washington, DC: U.S. Department of Justice.

Espy, M.W. & J.O. Smykla (1987). *Executions in the United States, 1608-1987: The Espy File* (codebook). Tuscaloosa, AL: J.O. Smykla (producer); Ann Arbor, MI: Inter-University Consortium for Political and Social Research (distributor).

Sellin, T. (1950). "A Note on Capital Executions in the United States." *British Journal of Delinquency,* 1(July):6-7.

Teeters, N.K. & C.J. Zibulka (1984). "Executions Under State Authority: An Inventory." In W.J. Bowers' *Legal Homicide,* pp. 395-525. Boston: Northeastern University Press.

U.S. Department of Commerce (1929). *Prisoners in State and Federal Reformatories, 1926 Summary.* Washington, DC: U.S. Government Printing Office.

U.S. Department of Interior (1864). *Compendium of the Eighth Census, 1860.* Washington, DC: U.S. Government Printing Office.

U.S. Department of Interior (1854). *Compendium of the Seventh Census, 1850.* Washington, DC: U.S. Government Printing Office.

U.S. Department of Interior (1888). *Dependent, Defective, and Delinquent Classes of the Population of the United States as Returned at the Tenth Census: 1880.* Washington, DC: U.S. Government Printing Office.

U.S. Department of Justice (1971). *National Prisoner Statistics Capital Punishment 1930-1970 Bulletin 46.* Washington, DC: U.S. Government Printing Office.

U.S. Department of Justice (1988). *Capital Punishment 1987.* Washington, DC: U.S. Government Printing Office.

2

The General Prevention Effect of Capital Punishment for Non-Capital Felonies

William C. Bailey
Cleveland State University

INTRODUCTION

It is probably fair to conclude that over the last decade and a half, few issues have received greater attention in criminology and criminal justice than the proper role of capital punishment in this society. This is evident in (1) the amount of attention devoted to the death penalty in leading criminology, criminal justice, law and social science journals, (2) the publication of dozens of recent books on the subject, (3) the number of death penalty issues brought before the state and federal appellate courts, and (4) a number of very important rulings by the United States Supreme Court since the mid-1970s. Indeed, recent years have witnessed greater legal and scholarly attention to the death penalty question than during any other period in our history.

Social scientists have played an important role in attempting to better understand factual issues pertaining to the death penalty, including: (1) the deterrent effect of capital punishment on murder, and (2) racial bias and discrimination in the administration of capital punishment. While deterrence and discrimination are significant theoretical and policy questions, other important issues also should be explored. Among them, is the possible preventive effects of the death penalty for crimes that are not capital offenses.

On the surface this question may seem superfluous. The deterrence argument rests upon the assumption that potential offenders are knowledgeable, rational, and calculating beings, who would disregard execution as a possible consequence of committing a non-capital offense such as rape, burglary, robbery, and auto theft. However, the works of Andenaes (1974), Lehtinen (1977), Gibbs (1978),

21

Berns (1979), van den Haag (1983), and Yunker (1982a, 1982b) provide reason to expect an inverse relationship between the level of capital punishment and non-capital offenses. The key lies in (1) the general preventive (normative validation, educative, and moralizing) effects of punishment, (2) "spill over" effects from deterring crimes where murder is not intended, but is a possible outcome, and (3) the system overload consequences that high levels of murder have on diverting criminal justice resources away from crime prevention and the successful adjudication of non-capital offenders.

General Prevention

Andenaes (1952, 1966, 1968, 1971, 1974, 1975) discusses the possible general preventive effects of legal punishment. He emphasizes the important role of the law and its application in helping to educate the public and in shaping moral judgments.[1] Echoing Durkheim (1949), he contends that society applies legal sanctions to wrongdoers to underscore the sanctity of life, limb, and property. In this respect, capital punishment may be unique among sanctions. Andenaes argues that these more subtle educative and moralizing effects of punishment may impact on both the conscious and subconscious levels, and may be quite general in their effect rather than tied to particular types of offenses. According to Lehtinen (1977:240-241):

> More than any other penalty, the death penalty reinforces the value of conformity to the law, whose ultimate authority is diffused into the subconscious of the citizenry.... The moral, pedagogical effects of the death penalty reinforce conformity to all law, not just the law of capital crimes.[2]

Although the effects of punishment may be rather general, it could be argued that the "message" sent out by the execution of a convicted murderer might have a greater preventive impact on some types of crime than others (i.e., crimes against persons than crimes against property).

Deterrence

In addition to the possible "moralizing," "educative," and "normative validation" effects of the death penalty, James Yunker (1982b:118) has argued that capital punishment may "deter" all serious offenses because "all serious crime represents a threat to life, even though the perpetrator may not 'want' to kill." He suggests that it is a fallacy to argue that "the death penalty only deters behavior that is inevitably murderous." Rather, the death penalty also deters behavior that merely tends to produce murder, that is, behavior that creates circumstances and conditions making the commission of a homicide likely" (118). For example, Yunker (1982a, 1982b) contends that capital punishment deters such diverse non-capital offenses as robbery, burglary, tavern fights, and wifebeating. In this context, it is important to recognize that a sizable proportion of homicides (20-25% annually, according to the FBI) involve other types of felonies, often referred to as felony-murders. Typically felony-murders are not planned killings. Rather, they start out as other types of crime but end up as lethal due to surprise, panic, and self-protective actions by victims and offenders.

Presently, no jurisdiction in the country prescribes the death penalty for any FBI index felony not involving homicide—robbery, rape, burglary, grand theft, vehicle theft and arson (U.S. Department of Justice, 1988). However, all death penalty jurisdictions provide for capital punishment for one or more types of felony-murder (Peterson & Bailey, 1988). And, historically as well as presently, the vast majority of persons sentenced to death have been convicted of felony-murder. Indeed, the capital murder problem in this country is largely a felony-murder problem. This being the case, it would not be unreasonable to expect that capital punishment might discourage felonies that often have a lethal outcome. Although Yunker's argument may have merit for all types of felony offenses, one would speculate that capital punishment would have a greater "deterrent" impact on person-to-person felonies such as robbery and rape, where victims and offenders come into physical contact, than on most larcenies, burglaries and auto thefts.

System Overload

A third way in which the death penalty may influence non-capital crimes is through the consequences of system overload. The concept of system overload refers to the negative effect that a high volume of crime has on the ability of criminal justice institutions (e.g., police, prosecutors, courts) to effectively carry out their jobs of preventing crime, and apprehending and adjudicating offenders. When the justice system becomes overloaded, it becomes less efficient in meeting its responsibilities. Indeed, the impact of a high volume of crime is to deter effective crime prevention and adjudication (Yunker, 1982a, 1982b). In defending capital punishment for murder, Yunker argues (1) that the reduced use of executions in the 1960s and 1970s caused an increase in homicides, (2) that diverted a greater share of police and judicial resources to the homicide problem, and (3) thereby reduced the chances of arrest and conviction for lesser crimes. According to Yunker, this reduced level of the certainty of punishment has provided an added incentive to commit non-capital crimes. Thus, for Yunker, the downturn in capital punishment has resulted in an increase in all serious crime in recent years.

In sum, then, it is theoretically possible that capital punishment could effect non-capital crimes through (1) moralization, normative validation, and related education effects, (2) deterring serious felonies because of the possibility of felony-murder and resulting execution, and (3) the effect that killings have on diverting criminal justice resources that influence the certainty and severity of punishment for other offenses. If any or all of these arguments are correct, we would expect a significant inverse relationship between the level of use of the death penalty and the rates of serious felonies.

Importantly, if this predicted inverse relationship is observed, there is no feasible way of separating the possible deterrent, general prevention, or system overload consequences of capital punishment (Gibbs, 1978; Brier & Fienberg, 1980). All one could conclude is that through at least one of the hypothesized processes (or some unknown means) executions influence non-capital crimes. From a theoretical point of view this uncertainty is unfortunate. However, from a policy standpoint, these distinctions may not be of major concern.

THE PRESENT INVESTIGATION

Despite the claims noted above regarding possible theoretical linkages between capital punishment and crime in general, my review of the law and criminology literature has failed to detect a single empirical analysis of the relationship between the death penalty and rates for non-capital crimes. The present chapter is an attempt to fill this void. To explore the possible preventive effects of the death penalty for non-capital crimes, I have borrowed from the methodologies of two types of deterrence studies: (1) investigations that have examined cross-sectionally for states the correspondence between crime rates for FBI index felonies and the certainty and severity of imprisonment for these offenses; and (2) investigations of the relationship between state execution rates and variation in homicide rates. Drawing upon these two bodies of research, the general model examined here is of the following form:

$$FR = (EXEC, CERT, SEV, CITY, AGE, NW, INEQ, UNP)$$

This model predicts that state felony rates (FR) for index crimes are a function of the level of execution for murder (EXEC), the certainty (CERT) and severity (SEV) of imprisonment for the felonies in question, percentage of the population residing in cities (CITY), percentage of the population 20-40 years of age (AGE), percentage of the population that is nonwhite (NW), the level of income inequality (INEQ), as measured by the Gini Index, and percentage of the civilian labor force that is unemployed (UNP). By including in the model various sociodemographic factors that have been found to be linked with felony rates, one is better able to isolate the effects of the sanction variables. Incorporating the certainty and severity of imprisonment in the model controls for their possible deterrent, incapacitation, and other preventive effects on felony rates (Gibbs, 1975). This enables us to better isolate the impact of executions on non-capital crimes. As noted above, I would expect a statistically significant inverse relationship between the level of use of capital punishment (execution rates) and rates for non-capital felonies, net of the effects of the control variables in the model.

Methods and Procedures

To test the model, required execution, offense, and sociodemographic data for death penalty states were gathered from various U.S. government sources for two years—1950 and 1960. For each year, state felony rates were drawn from the FBI's *Uniform Crime Reports*. For each state, the required sociodemographic figures were drawn from the decenial census volumes for 1950 and 1960. Execution and imprisonment figures came from reports issued by the Federal Bureau of Prisons.

For each index offense, severity of imprisonment is measured as the median number of months of imprisonment served by convicted felons released from prison in 1950 and 1960. The certainty of imprisonment is operationalized as (1) the number of prison admissions for each felony, for each state, for each year, divided by (2) the number of respective felonies for each state for each year. For ease of interpretation, the resulting certainty of imprisonment values are converted to percentages.

As Andenaes (1974, 1975) and Gibbs (1975, 1978) have pointed out, for any particular crime, the greater the certainty of a legal sanction, the greater its hypothesized deterrent and general prevention effects. However, theoretically and operationally, it is unclear what constitutes an appropriate measure of the certainty of execution. For example, should one consider (1) the ratio of yearly executions for murder to the total number of murders, (2) the ratio of the number of executions to the number of convicted murderers during that year, or (3), simply the sheer number of executions performed each year. In brief, the question is, what type of measure best reflects the hypothesized "anti-crime message" conveyed by executions?

Unfortunately, little attention has been paid to this question in the death penalty literature. In the absence of clear theoretical guidance, and since the present study is highly exploratory, I have chosen to consider the relationship between yearly offense rates and eight different execution measures:

(1) the ratio of the number of executions to homicides both for year t,
(2) the ratio of the number of executions for year t-1 to homicides for year t-1,
(3) the number of executions during year t,
(4) the number of executions during year t-1,
(5) the ratio of the number of executions during year t to the number of admissions to prison for homicide during year t,

(6) the ratio of the number of executions during year t to the number of admissions to prison for homicide during year t-1,

(7) the mean number of yearly executions for the previous ten-year period,

(8) the mean number of yearly executions for the previous twenty-year period.

With the exceptions of operationalizations 7 and 8, each of these measures has been considered in previous deterrence and death penalty studies. I add yearly executions for the previous 10- and 20-year periods to explore the possible long-term effects of executions on non-capital crimes.

Analysis

To test the models, the various execution measures, crime and socio-demographic data are incorporated into a series of multiple regression analyses. Eight index crimes (murder and nonnegligent manslaughter, negligent man-slaughter, assault, rape, robbery, burglary, larceny, auto theft) are considered for 1950. Only six offenses are examined for 1960. For this year, required imprison-ment figures are not available for rape or manslaughter. (Although the deterrent and general preventive effects of executions on murder have been researched thoroughly, I include the murder and nonnegligent manslaughter index offense in the analysis for comparative purposes.)

Although one might argue that the preventive effects of capital punishment may extend beyond major felonies, data constraints preclude expanding the anal-ysis to include other felonies and misdemeanors. For the periods under consider-ation, state-level crime rates and imprisonment figures needed to compute the certainty and severity of incarceration measures are available only for the index felonies.

Historical fact and data constraints also restrict the study to a cross-sectional analysis of death penalty jurisdictions for 1950 and 1960.[3] To provide a proper test of the impact of executions, it is important to examine a period where there is substantial use of capital punishment, but also variation in the levels of execu-tion across jurisdictions. This requirement rules out an examination of the second half of the 1960s, and the 1970s and 1980s because of the small number of executions.[4]

Executions were much more common during the earlier decades of this century. Importantly too, during earlier periods there was substantial variation in the use of capital punishment from jurisdiction to jurisdiction. I was unable to consider the first five decades of this century, however, because required execu-tion, crime rate, imprisonment, and sociodemographic data are not available. Crime, execution and limited imprisonment figures are available for some non-census years during the 1950s and early 1960s. However, important sociodemographic control variable data are limited to the 1950 and 1960 census years. Restricting the analysis to these two years does not pose a major limitation for examining the theoretical issues identified. If the death penalty does discourage non-capital crimes, it should be evident in an analysis of 1950 and 1960 execution and crime patterns.

Multicollinearity

To explore the possible problem of multicollinearity, the basic model was subjected to a series of auxiliary regressions for each year. This analysis indicated no significant collinearity problems for the execution measures. Neither individually nor in linear combination, were any of the other right-hand variables associated so closely with the execution measures as to yield inefficient results. In most cases, when the execution measures were regressed against the other factors, the resulting R^2 values ranged from .10 to .30. For 1950, for the models that considered the extended 10- and 20-year execution measures, the R^2 values reach the .55 to .60 level. However, even these values are not so large as to suggest a serious collinearity problem. It also should be emphasized that the concern in this study is with estimating the effect of executions on felony rates only. The other right-hand variables are introduced in the models only for statistical control purposes. Therefore, the interdependence among the imprisonment and sociodemographic factors is not of direct concern.

Table 2.1 Zero-Order Correlations Between Execution Measures and State Felony Rates

1950 Execution Measure	Murder	Man-slaughter	Assault	Rape	Robbery	Burglary	Larceny	Auto Theft
1. Execution Rt., Yr. t	.247	-.096	.027	.288a	.098	.052	.081	.270a
2. Execution Rt., Yr. t-1	.123	-.121	.015	.198	.111	.042	.127	.309a
3. No. of Executions, Yr. t	.223	-.030	.117	.215	.106	-.038	-.108	-.004
4. No. of Executions, Yr. t-1	.085	-.072	.153	.070	.015	-.114	-.089	-.070
5. Conditional Execution Rt., Yr. t	.107	-.112	-.008	.342a	.160	.084	.098	.342a
6. Conditional 1-yr. Lagged Execution Rate	-.102	-.129	-.145	.212	.055	.085	.208	.325a
7. 10-Yr. X̄ No. of Executions	.414b	-.016	.356a	.152	-.035	-.054	-.176	.017
8. 20-Yr. X̄ No. of Executions	.329a	-.039	.190	.087	-.014	-.116	-.233	-.003

1960 Execution Measure	Murder	Assault	Robbery	Burglary	Larceny	Auto Theft
1. Execution Rt., Yr. t	.009	-.113	-.083	.244	.297a	.202
2. Execution Rt., Yr. t-1	.017	-.028	-.158	-.139	-.138	-.134
3. No. of Executions, Yr. t	.158	.061	.093	.240	.269a	.128
4. No. of Executions, Yr. t-1	.152	.131	.123	.267a	.167	.042
5. Conditional Execution Rt., Yr. t	.035	-.121	.031	.367b	.385b	.319a
6. Conditional 1-Yr. Lagged Execution Rate	.025	.049	.232	.527c	.482c	.459c
7. 10-Yr. X̄ No. of Executions	.374b	.266	.224	.405b	.242	.161
8. 20-Yr. X̄ No. of Executions	.473c	.347	.111	.267	.108	.020

a=p<.05; b=p<.01; c=p<.001

FINDINGS

To reiterate, in light of deterrence, educative, and normative validation arguments, one would expect a significant negative relationship between the level of use of the death penalty in retentionist states (the number or rate of executions) and the rates of different types of felonies. Table 2.1 reports the bivariate associations between each execution measure and felony rates. The data in the top portion of the table pertain to 1950, and the lower half to 1960.

The top panel of Table 2.1 provides no indication that the number or rate of executions had a significant *negative* impact on felony rates for 1950. This holds regardless of the time lag and time period for executions. To the contrary, a majority of the bivariate correlations (40/64 = 63%) are positive, and some of the positive coefficients are statistically significant. The patterns for auto theft, and to a lesser extent rape, are most notable in this regard.

The bivariate patterns for 1960 are also contrary to expectations. Again, most of the correlations are positive (40/48 = 83%) rather than negative. Further, half of the positive correlations for burglary and larceny are statistically significant, as are two of the coefficients for murder and auto theft.

In brief, although the patterns for 1950 and 1960 differ somewhat, in both cases the results fail to support deterrence, general prevention, and system overload arguments for executions and non-capital crimes. However, the bivariate analyses do not indicate the *net effect* of executions on felony rates.

Table 2.2 Felony Rates Regressed Against Yearly Execution Rates, Certainty and Severity of Imprisonment and Selected Sociodemographic Variables

1950 Independent Variable	Murder	Man-slaughter	Assault	Rape	Robbery	Burglary	Larceny	Auto Theft
% City	.013	.107	1.376	−.065	.610a	−1.932	−4.714	.829
% Age 20-40 Yrs.	.001	.455	3.360	.092	1.662	13.523	34.521	3.732
% Nonwhite	.143	.023	5.291a	.028	−.719	1.684	−20.046	−2.893
Income Inequality	49.400a	16.419	680.806	9.268	47.183	983.805	194.159	500.867
% Unemployment	−.347	−.296	−10.425	.547	−.122	36.418	159.484	5.319
Certainty of Prison	−.003	−.032	−.575	−.108c	−.786b	−29.647	−125.368	−6.894
Severity of Prison	−.024	−.192	−1.156	−.073	−.652	−8.646	−15.115	.046
Execution Rt., Yr. t	.099	−.031	1.024	.380	1.815	7.871	7.502	−6.644
Constant	−9.507	−8.981	−250.146	9.042	3.640	−106.367	−91.581	−169.398
R^2	.542c	.126	.466b	.581c	.411a	.080	.204	.226

1960 Independent Variable	Murder	Assault	Robbery	Burglary	Larceny	Auto Theft
% City	−.021	1.466	.918b	3.987a	1.573	1.831
% Age 20-40 yrs.	.126	.725	.564	1.780	−6.207	−.898
% Nonwhite	.150c	3.394c	.518	.961	1.180	−.074
Income Inequality	61.087c	718.379c	−11.317	1896.680a	−523.934	−187.462
% Unemployment	−.046	−1.189	2.014	33.623	26.574	14.311
Certainty of Prison	−.040a	.152	−.941	−67.939b	−12.102	−4.632
Severity of Prison	−.018a	1.021	−.223	−12.151a	−3.853	3.564
Execution Rt., Yr. t	.379a	−3.720	−2.649	29.460	15.092	3.539
Constant	−16.710	−274.313	17.355	−164.436	507.426	74.724
R^2	.843c	.773c	.521b	.508b	.482b	.486a

a = $p<.05$; b = $p<.01$; c = $p<.001$

The top portion of Table 2.2 reports the results of the analysis where felony rates for 1950 are regressed against yearly execution rates for murder ((number of executions/number of reported murders)*100) and the other predictors in the model. The figures reported in Table 2.2 (and the tables to follow) are unstandardized partial regression coefficients. Again, I see no support for the deterrence, general prevention, and system overload hypotheses. For all but two offenses (manslaughter and auto theft), felony rates are associated positively with execution rates. Further, regardless of sign, there is a chance-only relationship between executions and felony rates for 1950.

Of interest, for each offense, the relationship between the certainty of imprisonment and offense rates is negative as predicted by deterrence theory, and for rape and robbery the coefficients are statistically significant. For each offense except auto theft, length of prison sentence is also negatively associated with rates, but none of the severity coefficients are significant.

The lower half of Table 2.2 reports a parallel analysis for 1960. As with 1950, a majority (4/6) of the execution coefficients are positive, and the positive coefficient for murder is statistically significant. Here, on average, a one percent increase in yearly execution rates is associated with about a four-tenths (b = .379) of a person increase in the homicide rate. This result is consistent with the notion that executions may actually promote homicides because of their "brutalization effect" (Bowers & Pierce, 1980). I will return to the "brutalization" question later in the analysis.

In a number of previous deterrence investigations, a time lag has been introduced in considering the relationship between sanction variables and offense rates. The rationale is that sanctions may have a delayed deterrent effect that cannot be detected when executions and murder rates are examined within the same year. To explore this possibility for executions and non-capital crimes, the analyses reported in Table 2.2 are repeated but for yearly (year t) offense rates, and execution rates for the previous year (year t-1).[5]

These analyses also produce no evidence that executions influence non-capital felonies. For neither year is there other than a chance association between executions and offense rates. Thus, there is no indication that executions have a delayed deterrent, general prevention, or system overload (or brutalization) effect on felony rates.

Thus far, I have relied upon *rates* of execution in examining the influence of the certainty of the death penalty on non-capital offenses. The operating assumption has been that the more certain the sanction, the more effective the "anti-crime" message, whether it is through fear (deterrence), education, or moral persuasion (normative validation). It is possible, however, that the public's perception of the certainty of sanctions, including execution, is not well measured by the objective certainty of punishment. A knowledgeable public may maintain a fairly accurate running count of the number of homicides and resulting executions. However, it is more likely that the general public has only a vague awareness of the murder count. Most persons probably perceive the level of murder in very general terms, such as being "high," "increasing," and the like.

If the public has only a vague awareness of the murder count (which is the denominator of the previously used execution rate measures), then the *number*, rather than the *rate* of executions, may be a more appropriate indicator of the public's perception of the certainty of the death penalty. To explore this possibility, I now consider the sheer number of executions as an additional indicator of the certainty of the death penalty.

Table 2.3 reports the results of the analysis where yearly felony rates for 1950 are regressed against the number of executions during the year and the other right-hand variables. The 1960 analysis is presented in the lower half of the table.

Table 2.3 Felony Rates Regressed Against the Yearly Number of Executions, Certainty and Severity of Imprisonment and Selected Sociodemographic Variables

1950 Independent Variable	Murder	Man-slaughter	Assault	Rape	Robbery	Burglary	Larceny	Auto Theft
% City	.003	.125	1.300	−.085	.482	−2.215	−4.695	.847
% Age 20-40 Yrs.	.030	.472	3.778	.090	1.833	10.905	25.356	3.838
% Nonwhite	.146	.056	5.270a	.048	−.575	3.030	−16.590	−3.112
Income Inequality	50.535a	21.909	671.423	15.016	52.313	1177.197	1149.406	410.902
% Unemployment	−.294	−.174	−10.330	.851	−.959	48.957	187.147	4.060
Certainty of Prison	−.002	−.035	−.574	−.110c	−.739b	−30.382	−140.259	−6.539
Severity of Prison	−.021	−.178	−1.361	−.019	−.688	−7.402	−7.649	−.027
# Executions, Yr. t	.185	−.567	2.239	.031	1.271	−16.102	−63.998	−.389
Constant	−11.308	−12.381	−253.724	−4.782	−3.531	−142.159	−329.157	−138.537
R²	.542c	.139	.467b	.528b	.378a	.081	.216	.184

1960 Independent Variable	Murder	Assault	Robbery	Burglary	Larceny	Auto Theft
% City	−.019	1.506	.906b	3.530	1.484	1.897
% Age 20-40 yrs.	.187a	.378	.664	8.326	−4.605	−1.420
% Nonwhite	.147c	3.422c	.523	1.166	1.113	−.154
Income Inequality	58.089c	753.445c	2.806	1686.005	−727.598	−134.923
% Unemployment	.047	−.872	1.614	34.038	26.389	16.530
Certainty of Prison	−.034a	.165	−.924	−76.185b	−11.085	−4.141
Severity of Prison	−.014	.841	−.204	−13.687a	−3.345	3.390
# Executions, Yr. t	.217	−1.472	.263	24.849	6.821	−1.063
Constant	−18.029		8.626	−179.388	541.117	60.746
R²	.831c	.767c	.508b	.503b	.447a	.484a

a = p<.05; b = p<.01; c = p<.001

Table 2.3 gives no evidence that executions significantly reduced felony rates in 1950. For half of the offenses, the trade-off between executions and felony rates is negative and for the other half the association is positive. In each case, the relationship is only at a chance level. The results for 1960 are equally at odds with the deterrence and general prevention arguments. The execution coefficients are mixed in sign, and none differ significantly from zero. Although not shown here, the same pattern holds for 1950 and 1960 when the number of executions lagged by one year (year t-1) is substituted for the yearly (year t) number of executions.

Conditional Executions

To this point there is no indication that executions have an immediate or delayed preventive effect on non-capital felonies, regardless of whether the certainty of the death penalty is operationalized as (1) the ratio of executions to murders, or simply (2) the number of executions. I now consider an additional measure of the certainty of execution—the conditional probability of an execution. Table 2.4 reports the results of the analysis for 1950 and 1960 where the certainty of execution is measured by (1) the number of executions for murder during the year, divided by (2) the number of prison admissions for murder during the year. It is possible that public perceptions of the certainty of execution are based upon the disposition pattern for convicted murderers—the proportion put to death.

Table 2.4 Felony Rates Regressed Against Yearly Conditional Execution Rates, Certainty and Severity of Imprisonment and Selected Sociodemographic Variables

1950 Independent Variable	Murder	Man-slaughter	Assault	Rape	Robbery	Burglary	Larceny	Auto Theft
% City	-.018	.104	1.301	-.069	.613	-1.878	-4.954	.824
% Age 20-40 Yrs.	-.008	.452	3.378	.090	1.714	13.802	34.802	3.614
% Nonwhite	.132	.028	5.385^a	.025	-.759	1.427	-19.745	-2.888
Income Inequality	51.196	15.591	685.742	14.493	76.567	1104.676	333.383	402.341
% Unemployment	-.352	-.276	-9.496	.740	.525	39.556	164.490	3.828
Certainty of Prison	-.002	-.032	-.611	-.104^c	-.752^b	-29.184	-126.641	-7.063
Severity of Prison	-.024	-.187	-1.169	-.072	-.664	-8.643	-15.176	.125
Conditional Exec. Rt.	.101	-.045	-.083	.209	1.181	4.931	2.115	-2.778
Constant	-10.735	-8.663	-251.976	6.027	-13.548	-182.898	-161.200	-122.299
R^2	.551^c	.127	.465^b	.567^c	.415^a	.081	.204	.200

1960 Independent Variable	Murder	Assault	Robbery	Burglary	Larceny	Auto Theft
% City	-.024	1.526^b	.922^b	3.438	1.266	1.751
% Age 20-40 yrs.	.126	.744	.588	1.876	-6.155	-.828
% Nonwhite	.160^c	3.322^c	.499	1.769	1.698	.119
Income Inequality	60.333^c	728.759^c	2.784	1719.067	-540.108	-206.472
% Unemployment	-.051	-.620	1.807	31.181	24.406	13.687
Certainty of Prison	-.036^a	.150	-.930	-66.296^b	-12.542	-4.449
Severity of Prison	-.018^a	.836	-.214	-10.274	-3.113	3.665
Conditional Exec. Rt.	.187^a	-1.455	-.415	15.869^a	9.022^a	2.710
Constant	-16.520	-279.699	10.549	-120.922	516.288	81.361
R^2	.848^c	.771^c	.509^b	.529^b	.516^b	.492^a

a = p<.05; b = p<.01; c = p<.001

If the public is sensitive to this ratio, one would expect the conditional probability of execution and felony rates to be negatively and significantly associated. This is not the case, however. For 1950, for five of the eight offenses, these two factors are positively associated, and regardless of direction, none of the coefficients is statistically significant.

For 1960, the results are also contrary to predictions. Indeed, Table 2.4 shows that there is a significant positive relationship between the conditional probability of execution and rates of murder, burglary and larceny. For the other three offenses, the trade-off between executions and rates is only at a chance level.

The significant positive association between conditional execution rates and the murder rate is consistent with the hypothesized brutalization effect of capital punishment. However, it is difficult to imagine how such a brutalization effect could spill over to property offenses like burglary and larceny, when there is *no evidence* of such an effect for the person-to-person crimes of assault and robbery. Moreover, why would executions have a brutalization effect for some offenses in 1960, but not for the same offenses in 1950?

An alternative explanation of the significant positive relationship between conditional execution rates for 1960 and rates of murder, burglary and larceny is that the level of crime effects the *demand for executions*. However, there is typically a delay of at least one year or longer between the sentencing and execution of convicted murderers. Accordingly, it is difficult to see how (1) offense rates for 1960 could influence in a positive direction (2) the ratio of executions to the number of prison admissions for murder that same year. Further, why would the level for the property crimes of burglary and larceny influence the demand for executions, when the more feared person-to-person crimes of assault and robbery do not?

It is possible that the public is aware of the typical time lag between imprisonment and possible execution, and perceives the certainty of execution in this manner. To explore this question, a one-year lagged conditional execution rate was considered: the ratio of (1) the number of executions during the year (year t) to (2) the number of prison admissions for murder during the previous year (year t-1).

My test of this question does not yield support for the general prevention hypothesis. Again, there is only a chance positive or negative association between lagged conditional execution rates and felony rates for 1950. For 1960, the association between these two factors is statistically significant, but in a positive direction for burglary ($b = 38.451$, $p < .01$), larceny ($b = 18.293$, $p < .01$), and auto theft ($b = 21.930$, $p < .05$). There is no obvious explanation of these surprising findings. However, they clearly are contrary to deterrence, general prevention, and system overload expectations.

Crime Rates and Long-Term Execution Trends

The results of the analysis of the possible "short-term" impact of executions on felony rates have been uniformly negative. It may be a mistake, however, to expect that execution practices will have an immediate (within the year, or during the next year) impact on offense rates. Andenaes (1974), for example, argues that the moralizing and educative effects of the law are long-term. Similarly, it might be argued that the public's perception of the certainty of legal sanctions and their possible effect is not based upon current or immediate criminal justice practices, but rather upon practices over a more extended period. Accordingly, it seems advisable to examine long-term state execution patterns.

To do so, felony rates for 1950 and 1960 were regressed against the respective sociodemographic and imprisonment variables and the average number of annual executions for 10- and 20-year periods: 1941-1950 for 1950, and 1951-1960 for 1960. Results of the 10-year analyses for 1950 and 1960 are reported in Table 2.5.

Table 2.5 Felony Rates Regressed Against Ten-Year Average Yearly Executions, Certainty and Severity of Imprisonment and Selected Sociodemographic Variables

1950 Independent Variable	Murder	Man-slaughter	Assault	Rape	Robbery	Burglary	Larceny	Auto Theft
% City	−.004	.138	1.158	−.104	.547	−1.551	−.741	.700
% Age 20-40 Yrs.	−.005	.572	3.238	.087	1.936	14.884	54.317	3.531
% Nonwhite	.183	−.007	6.947^b	.056	−.676	3.210	−26.269	−2.423
Income Inequality	58.811	20.203	1059.951^a	12.196	66.041	1584.768	2354.428	532.654
% Unemployment	−.216	−.540	−11.175	.738	.512	42.262	143.224	3.134
Certainty of Prison	−.004	−.032	−.514	−.108^c	−.813^b	−30.250	−186.646	−6.341
Severity of Prison	−.017	−.209	−1.214	−.050	−.688	−10.425	−30.944	−.648
X̄ Executions	.102	−.267	1.024	.186	−.004	−10.280	−32.864	.697
Constant	−14.095	−12.418	−380.104	7.686	−6.918	−335.194	−1042.143	−159.199
R^2	.527^b	.143	.582^c	.545^b	.388	.082	.235	.222

1960 Independent Variable	Murder	Assault	Robbery	Burglary	Larceny	Auto Theft
% City	−.033	1.073^a	.857^a	3.469	1.351	1.930
% Age 20-40 Yrs.	.143	−.760	.707	5.745	−5.942	−.907
% Nonwhite	.182^c	4.602^c	.575	1.224	1.382	−.360
Income Inequality	64.360^c	978.308^c	−.349	1436.630	−728.116	−208.720
% Unemployment	.151	.546	1.534	35.930	26.730	14.253
Certainty of Prison	−.026	.119	−.921	−66.780^b	−9.851	−4.269
Severity of Prison	−.012	.904	−.203	−14.555^a	−3.415	3.292
X̄ Executions	.255	−1.570	1.020	28.642a	5.269	−.777
Constant	−19.981	−325.119	9.054	−62.996	573.465	84.033
R^2	.857^c	.841^c	.503^b	.526^b	.407^a	.479^a

a = p<.05; b = p<.01; c = p<.001

To reiterate, the expectation is that the greater the number of executions over an extended period (10 years), the greater the deterrent and normative validation effects of capital punishment. Table 2.5 provides no indication that this is the case for 1950. The execution coefficients are mixed in sign, and none are statistically significant. For 1960, the same pattern holds with one exception. For burglary, average executions are positively and significantly ($p<.05$) associated with offense rates.

The consideration of a ten-year period of executions does not rest upon a theory of how long it takes for the preventive effects of sanctions to be realized. It is possible that the moralizing, educative and normative validation effects of capital punishment are not captured by examining a single decade.

To explore this question, I repeated the analyses shown in Table 2.5, but substituted average yearly executions for murder for 20-year periods (1931-1950 and 1941-1960). A 20-year period covers most of the life span of the age groups that were most heavily involved in index felonies in 1950 and 1960 (FBI, 1951, 1961).

Extending the period of executions to two decades does not alter the basic pattern of results. For both 1950 and 1960, felony rates are negatively associated with executions for some offenses and positively for others, but in no case does the association differ significantly from zero. Because the results of the 20-year analysis parallels so closely the earlier findings (Table 2.5), I have not presented these findings in tabular form.

SUMMARY AND CONCLUSION

Traditionally, the crime prevention issue concerning the death penalty has been the deterrent effect of capital punishment on murder. This makes sense because historically in the United States, murder (and to a lesser degree kidnapping, rape, and treason) has been the focus of most death penalty legislation (Bowers, 1984). Presently 37 states prescribe capital punishment for various forms of homicide, while the death penalty is available in a few jurisdictions for other crimes.[6] The evidence emerging from over two centuries of research casts serious doubt that capital punishment is an effective deterrent to murder (Zimring & Hawkins, 1986).

Drawing upon the arguments of Andenaes (1974), Lehtinen (1977), van den Haag (1978) and Berns (1979), this chapter examines an alternative question regarding the role of capital punishment in this society; namely, its crime prevention effects on non-capital offenses. In discussing the possible general preventive effects of capital punishment, these writers advance the argument that the major impact of the law and its application is to "socialize," "educate," and "moralize" society. These more subtle processes are believed to be far more important than deterrence in contributing to an orderly social life.

Yunker (1982a, 1982b) also has argued that capital punishment may influence (promote or prevent) non-capital crimes through two different processes—deterrence and system overload. He contends that the death penalty deters crimes that have murder as a possible outcome, and consequently our refusal to execute killers has encouraged life-threatening crimes. Yunker further argues that as a result of our refusal to execute, there has been an increase in murders. This increase has diverted scarce criminal justice resources so as to make other types of crime more profitable due to reduced levels of apprehension and punishment.

Although different processes are seen as operative, the works of the above noted scholars lead to a common expectation: there should be a significant inverse relationship between the level of use of capital punishment and rates for non-capital felonies. The present analysis provides no support for this prediction. To the contrary, I have not observed at the bivariate (Table 2.1) or multivariate (Tables 2.2–2.5) level a single instance of a significant negative relationship between the level of use of capital punishment and index felony rates for 1950 and 1960. This pattern holds for the traditional targeted offense of murder, the person crimes of negligent manslaughter, rape, assault, and robbery, as well as the property crimes of burglary, grand larceny, and vehicle theft. In other words, there is no evidence for 1950 and 1960 that residents of death penalty jurisdictions are afforded an added measure of protection against serious crimes by executions. Rather, there appears to be no clear relationship, one way or the other, between the level of use of capital punishment and felony crime rates.

While this analysis has not supported the hypotheses advanced, it should not be concluded that punishment has no effects on crime. This investigation does not question the premise that the criminal law and its application may have a significant deterrent effect on some offenses. Similarly, the threat and the application of the law may serve to educate and reinforce in the public's mind the distinction between right and wrong, and thereby influence levels of conformity. And, due to "system overload," high levels of crime may deter punishment, and thereby encourage crime. Based on my analysis, however, none of these processes seem to pertain to capital punishment and non-capital felonies.

NOTES

[1]   See Berkowitz and Walker (1967), Cohen (1971), Fienberg (1972), Zimring and Hawkins (1973), and Gibbs (1975, 1978) for parallel arguments on how the presence and application of the law (as well as the non-enforcement of the law) can influence levels of conformity via "enculturation," "moralization," and related socializing but non-threat processes.

[2]   Walter Berns (1979) and Ernest van den Haag (1978) make similar arguments in pointing to the significance of capital punishment as a means of maintaining respect for the law and expressing collective denunciation of crime irrespective of deterrence.

For example, according to van den Haag (1978) our "failure of nerve" (failure to execute) does serious damage to the moral solidarity of the community.

[3] The analysis excludes the following states that were without capital punishment for common murder in 1960: Rhode Island, Delaware, Wisconsin, Maine, Minnesota, North Dakota, Alaska and Hawaii. The 1950 analysis includes Delaware, which was then a retentionist jurisdiction. Alaska and Hawaii (retentionist jurisdictions until 1957) are excluded from the 1950 analysis because neither was a state that year.

[4] Accurate figures on the number of executions performed under civil authority are only available for the United States from 1930, the year when federal authorities began collecting execution data on a systematic basis. For five-year periods since 1930, the number of executions are as follows: 1930-1934 (776), 1935-1939 (891), 1940-1944 (645), 1945-1949 (639), 1950-1954 (413), 1955-1959 (304), 1960-1964 (181), 1965-1969 (10), 1970-1974 (0), 1975-1979 (3), 1980-1984 (29), 1985-1987 (61). For the years under investigation, there were 82 executions in 1950 and 56 in 1960 (Flanagan & Jamieson, 1988).

[5] The results for the lagged (year t-1) execution rate variables are similar enough to the non-lagged analysis (Table 2.2) that nothing would be gained by presenting them in tabular form. However, tables are available upon request.

[6] In addition to certain forms of murder, the following are capital offenses in the respective jurisdictions: aircraft piracy in Alabama, Georgia, and Mississippi; aggravated kidnapping or kidnapping for ransom in Montana, South Dakota, and Vermont; the rape of a child by an adult in Mississippi; and train wrecking in California (Bureau of Justice Statistics, 1988).

REFERENCES

Andenaes J. (1952). "General Prevention—Illusion or Reality?" *Journal of Criminal Law, Criminology and Police Science*, 43:176-198.

_____ (1966). "The General Preventive Effects of Punishment." *University of Pennsylvania Law Review*, 114:949-983.

_____ (1968). "Does Punishment Deter Crime?" *Criminal Law Quarterly*, 11:76-93.

_____ (1971). "The Moral or Educative Influence of Criminal Law." *Journal of Social Issues*, 27:17-31.

_____ (1974). *Punishment and Deterrence*. Ann Arbor: University of Michigan Press.

_____ (1975). "General Prevention Revisited: Research and Policy Implications." *Journal of Criminal Law and Criminology*, 66:338-365.

Berkowitz, L. & N. Walker (1967). "Laws and Moral Judgments." *Sociometry*, 30:410-422.

Berns, W. (1979). *For Capital Punishment.* New York: Basic Books.

Bowers, W.J. & G.L. Pierce (1980). "Deterrence or Brutalization: What is the Effect of Executions?" *Crime and Delinquency,* 26:453-484.

Brier, S.S. & S.E. Fienberg (1980). "Recent Econometric Modeling of Crime and Punishment." *Evaluation Review,* 4:147-191.

Cohen, M.R. (1971). "Moral Aspects of Punishment." In L. Radzinowicz & M.E. Wolfgang (eds.) *Crime and Justice,* Vol. III, 27-42. New York: Basic Books.

Durkheim, E. (1949). *Division of Labor in Society.* New York: Free Press.

Fienberg, J. (1972). "The Expressive Function of Punishment." In G. Ezorsky (ed.) *Crime and Personality,* 25-34. Boston: Houghton Mifflin.

Flanagan, T.J. & K.M. Jamieson (eds.) (1988). *Sourcebook of Criminal Justice Statistics—1987.* U.S. Department of Justice, Bureau of Justice Statistics. Washington, DC: U.S. Government Printing Office.

Gibbs, J.P. (1975). *Crime, Punishment and Deterrence.* New York: Elsevier.

_____ (1978). "Preventive Effects of Capital Punishment Other than Deterrence." *Criminal Law Bulletin,* 14:34-50.

Lehtinen, M. (1977). "The Voice of Life: An Argument for the Death Penalty. *Crime and Delinquency,* 23:237-252.

Peterson, R.D. & W.C. Bailey (1988). "Felony Murder and Capital Punishment." Paper presented at the annual meetings of the American Society of Criminology, Chicago.

Sellin, T. (1955). *The Royal Commission on Capital Punishment, 1949-1953. Report of the Great Britain Parliament.* (Papers by Command 8932). H.M. Stationery Office, pp. 17-24.

_____ (1961). "Capital Punishment." *Federal Probation,* 25:3-11.

_____ (1967). *Capital Punishment.* New York: Harper and Row.

_____ (1980). *The Penalty of Death.* Beverly Hills: Sage.

U.S. Department of Justice, Bureau of Justice Statistics (1988). *Capital Punishment 1987.* Washington, DC: U.S. Department of Justice, Bureau of Justice Statistics.

U.S. Department of Justice, Federal Bureau of Investigation (1951). *Uniform Crime Reports for the United States and Its Possessions—1950.* Washington, DC: U.S. Government Printing Office.

_____ (1961). *Uniform Crime Reports for the United States—1960.* Washington, DC: U.S. Government Printing Office.

van den Haag, E. (1978). "In Defense of the Death Penalty: A Legal-Practical-Moral Analysis." *Criminal Law Bulletin,* 14:51-68.

Yunker, J. (1982a). "Testing the Deterrent Effect of Capital Punishment: A Reduced Form Approach." *Criminology,* 19:626-644.

_____ (1982b). "The Relevance of the Identification Problem to Statistical Research on Capital Punishment." *Crime and Delinquency,* 28:96-124.

Zimring, F.E. & G. Hawkins (1973). *Deterrence: The Legal Threat in Crime Control.* Chicago: University of Chicago Press.

_____ (1986). *Capital Punishment and the American Agenda.* New York: Cambridge University Press.

3

Prosecutorial Discretion and Capital Sentencing In North and South Carolina

Raymond Paternoster
Institute of Criminal Justice and Criminology
University of Maryland

INTRODUCTION

The capital sentencing statutes of North and South Carolina have followed a similar history. For many years prior to the United States Supreme Court's decision in *Furman v. Georgia* (408 U.S. 238, 1972) both states allotted virtually unregulated discretion to the sentencing authority in determining which capital defendants should live and which should die. These "total discretion" statutes were, of course, struck down by the *Furman* decision, which declared that such schemes fail to provide a "meaningful basis for distinguishing the few cases in which [capital punishment] is imposed from the many cases in which it is not" (408 U.S. at 313, White, J., concurring). In response to *Furman*'s requirement that capital sentencing be more consistent in order to pass constitutional muster, the legislatures of both North and South Carolina passed new capital statutes which eliminated sentencing discretion by making the imposition of death mandatory upon conviction of newly created categories of first degree murder.

These mandatory statutes were, however, to meet the same constitutional fate, but for a different reason, as the pre-*Furman* legislation. The North Carolina statute was reviewed in *Woodson v. North Carolina* (428 U.S. 280, 1976) where the United States Supreme Court held that such mandatory statutes were unconstitutional because they failed "to allow the particularized consideration of relevant aspects of the character of each convicted defendant" (428 U.S. 280 at 303). Subsequent to the Court's ruling in *Woodson,* the South Carolina Supreme Court, in *State v. Rumsey,* (267 S.C. 236, 226 S.E.2d 894, 1976) declared its mandatory statute unconstitutional. Following the guidance of the United States Supreme Court in *Gregg v. Georgia* (428 U.S. 153, 1976) the state legislatures of North and South

Carolina constructed guided discretion capital sentencing statutes.

GUIDED DISCRETION STATUTES IN NORTH AND SOUTH CAROLINA

The guided discretion statutes passed in North and South Carolina, both of which became effective in June of 1977, were modeled after similar statutes operative in Florida and Georgia which had been approved by the United States Supreme Court (see, *Gregg v. Georgia* and *Proffitt v. Florida* 428 U.S. 242, 1976). As the title implies, these statutes attempt not to eliminate sentencer discretion, but to structure and guide its operation. This is achieved by requiring the sentencing authority to affirmatively find the existence of an enumerated statutory aggravating circumstance, and implicitly or explicitly weighing this against statutory and nonstatutory mitigating circumstances proffered in favor of a life sentence. The capital sentencing statutes of both North and South Carolina enumerate both aggravating and mitigating circumstances, and require the sentencer to weigh both factors before imposing sentence. Table 3.1 lists the statutory aggravating and mitigating circumstances in North and South Carolina applicable under the statutes constructed in 1977.

Table 3.1 Statutory Aggravating and Mitigating Factors in the Capital Sentencing Schemes of North and South Carolina

---

North Carolina

Aggravating Factors
(1)   The capital felony was committed by a person lawfully incarcerated.
(2)   The defendant had been previously convicted of another capital felony.
(3)   The defendant had been previously convicted of a felony involving the use or threat of violence to the person.
(4)   The capital felony was committed for the purpose of avoiding or preventing a lawful arrest or effecting an escape from custody.
(5)   The capital felony was committed while the defendant was engaged, or was an aider or abettor, in the commission of, or an attempt to commit, or flight after committing or attempting to commit, any robbery, rape or sex offense, arson, burglary, kidnapping, or aircraft piracy or the unlawful throwing, placing, or discharging of a destructive device or bomb.
(6)   The capital felony was committed for pecuniary gain.
(7)   The capital felony was committed to disrupt or hinder the lawful exercise of any governmental function or the enforcement of laws.
(8)   The capital felony was committed against a law enforcement officer, employee of the Department of Correction, jailer, fireman, judge or justice,

former judge or justice, prosecutor or former prosecutor, juror or former juror, or witness or former witness against the defendant, while engaged in the performance of his official duties because of the exercise of his official duty.

(9)   The capital felony was especially heinous, atrocious, or cruel.

(10)   The defendant knowingly created a great risk of death to more than one person by means of a weapon or device which would normally be hazardous to the lives of more than one person.

(11)   The murder for which the defendant stands convicted was part of a course of conduct in which the defendant engaged and which included the commission by the defendant of other crimes of violence against another person or persons.

Mitigating Factors

(1)   The defendant has no significant history of prior criminal activity.

(2)   The capital felony was committed while the defendant was under the influence of mental or emotional disturbance.

(3)   The victim was a voluntary participant in the defendant's homicidal conduct or consented to the homicidal act.

(4)   The defendant was an accomplice in or accessory to the capital felony committed by another person and his participation was relatively minor.

(5)   The defendant acted under duress or under the domination of another person.

(6)   The capacity of the defendant to appreciate the criminality of his conduct or to conform his conduct to the requirements of law was impaired.

(7)   The age of the defendant at the time of the crime.

(8)   The defendant aided in the apprehension of another capital felon or testified truthfully on behalf of the prosecution in another prosecution of a felony.

(9)   Any other circumstance arising from the evidence which the jury deems to have mitigating value.

South Carolina

Aggravating Factors

(1)   Murder was committed while in the commission of the following crimes or acts: (a) rape, (b) assault with intent to ravish, (c) kidnapping, (d) burglary, (e) robbery while armed with a deadly weapon, (f) larceny with use of a deadly weapon, (g) housebreaking, (h) killing by poison and (i) physical torture.

(2)   Murder was committed by a person with a prior record of conviction for murder.

(3)   The offender by his act of murder knowingly created a great risk of death to more than one person in a public place by means of a weapon or device which would normally be hazardous to the lives of more than one person.

(4)   The offender committed the offense of murder for himself or another, for the purpose of receiving money or any other thing of monetary value.

(5)   The murder of a judicial officer, former judicial officer, solicitor, former solicitor, or other officer of the court during or because of the exercise of his official duty.

(6)   The offender caused or directed another to commit murder or committed murder as an agent or employee of another person.

(7)   The offense of murder was committed against any peace officer, corrections employee or fireman while engaged in the performance of his official duties.

Mitigating Factors

(1)   The defendant had no significant history of prior criminal conviction involving the use of violence against another person.

(2)   The murder was committed while the defendant was under the influence of mental or emotional disturbance.

(3)   The victim was a participant in the defendant's conduct or consented to the act.

(4)   The defendant was an accomplice in the murder committed.

(5)   The defendant acted under duress or under the domination of another person.

(6)   The capacity of the defendant to appreciate the criminality of his conduct or to conform his conduct to the requirements of law was substantially impaired.

(7)   The age or mentality of the defendant at the time of the crime.

(8)   The defendant was provoked by the victim into committing the murder.

(9)   The defendant was below the age of eighteen at the time of the crime.

Source: N.C. Gen. Stat. Sec. 15A-2000(e)-(f) (1978 & Supp. 1979), S.C. Code Sec. 16-3-20 (C)(a)(b) (Supp. 1981).

As can be seen from Table 3.1, although there are some important differences between the two states in terms of specific aggravating and mitigating circumstances, there is substantial similarity and overlap.[1] In addition to these similarities, the statutes of both states require unanimous jury verdicts before a sentence of death may be imposed, the jury's recommendation of life is binding on the court in both states, and in both there is automatic direct appeal to the state supreme court. The latter is to ensure the factual accuracy of the sentence, its proportionality when compared with other cases, and whether the sentence of death was the product of passion or prejudice.

There is one additional similarity between the capital sentencing schemes of North and South Carolina, which is the central focus of this paper. In both states, the power to charge an offense as a capital murder, thereby making a homicide defendant statutorily eligible for the death penalty, is solely in the hands of the local prosecutor. In determining for which cases the penalty of death should be sought, neither the North nor South Carolina statute attempts to guide or restrict the discretion of the prosecutor. In both states the prosecutor is simply instructed to notify the defense in advance of trial if and for which aggravating factors the death penalty will be sought. In making the choice to seek a life or death sentence, neither the state supreme court nor statute requires the prosecutor to provide reasons, monitor the cases, or provide any sort of proportionality review. State courts and the United States Supreme Court apparently believed that the same aggravating and mitigating factors which guided and structured the discretion of the jury would "filter down" and inform the charging decision of the prosecutor: "Unless prosecutors are incompetent in their judgments, the standards by which they decide whether to charge a capital felony will be the same as those by which the jury will decide the questions of guilt and sentence" (*Gregg v. Georgia*, 428 U.S. 198, 1976 at 225).

Since prosecutors possess such unfettered discretion in making the charging decision it is an ideal decision point to study the effect of extralegal factors. In addition, it is important from a public policy perspective since the extensive doctrinal reform of capital sentencing undertaken by the United States Supreme Court since 1976 may be undermined if discretion is unwisely exercised at an earlier decision-making point in the system, untouched by such reforms. The specific purpose of this paper is to examine the factors that influence the decision of the prosecutor to seek the death penalty in North and South Carolina. Of particular interest will be the influence of race and the geographic location of the homicide. Since these two states are contiguous, have a similar historical and cultural tradition, and have followed very similar paths in drafting capital punishment statutes, it will be interesting to see if the administration of capital punishment within the jurisdiction of local prosecutors is similar. For the most part, previous research on the administration of post-*Furman* capital punishment statutes has been undertaken in geographically scattered states with little or no attempt to offer a comparison between states.

METHODS

South Carolina Data Sources

Data from South Carolina were collected by the author as part of a larger study of capital sentencing in that state (see, Paternoster, 1983; Paternoster & Kazyaka, 1988). An original data set was constructed which contained the Supplemental Homicide Report (SHR) for each of the approximately 1,800 non-negligent homicides committed in South Carolina from June 8, 1977 (the enactment date of the guided discretion capital statute) until December 31, 1981. Of these homicides, 311 (18%) were thought to have included an aggravating circumstance listed in the South Carolina statute. In 302 of these 311 "death eligible" murders the statutory aggravating circumstance was the commission of a contemporaneous felony. These 302 felony-type murder cases constitute the final pool of capital murders for subsequent analyses.

In addition to the SHR, information on these 302 felony-murder cases was obtained from the original police report of the homicide, any subsequent police investigation report, court and trial information kept by the Office of the Court's Administrator, and criminal history ("rap sheet") data from the files of those defendants eventually placed under the custody of the state department of corrections. From these diverse data sources a fairly detailed description of the homicide could be reconstructed, along with information about the victim(s), the defendant(s), and subsequent legal proceedings. Since local prosecutors are required to officially file with the court a formal notification to seek the death penalty 30 days prior to trial, a complete list of all those cases which resulted in a death penalty request could be obtained. In subsequent analyses the dependent variable is a binary one, the decision of the prosecutor to seek a sentence of death ("no" = 0; "yes" = 1).

South Carolina prosecutors clearly exercised their discretion in seeking a death sentence. Of 302 homicides that were statutorily eligible for capital punishment, a death sentence was sought in only 114 (38%). The data analyses reported in subsequent sections of this paper attempt to discover those factors that were most influential in this discretionary decision, and to determine if either the offender or victim's race was one such consideration.

North Carolina Data Sources

Data concerning prosecutorial charging decisions in North Carolina came from a study of capital sentencing in that state conducted by Barry Nakell. The author obtained Nakell's original data which included all homicides committed during the first year of North Carolina's guided discretion capital statute (from June 1, 1977 to May 31, 1978). Nakell's data set is described in more detail in his book (Nakell & Hardy, 1987), and the interested reader is referred to this source. For present purposes it is sufficient to note that he obtained information from the office of the medical examiner, police reports, court reports, and interviews with both prosecuting and defense attorneys. This information enabled him to classify each homicide according to important legal criteria, including the culpability of the defendant, the existence of mitigating and self-defense factors, the strength of the prosecution's case, the extent of the egregiousness of the homicide, and characteristics of both the victim and offender. For more detail concerning the data and the construction of the various scales used in subsequent analyses reported here, the reader is again referred to the Nakell and Hardy text.

During the first year of the administration of the state's new death penalty statute, there were approximately 650 homicides committed in North Carolina. All those cases that did not result in an arrest and an indictment were then excluded from further analysis, as were the handful of cases where the race of the victim or defendant was either unknown or was other than black or white. This resulted in a final pool of 468 homicides. Similar to their counterparts in South Carolina, North Carolina prosecutors exercised considerable discretion in deciding to seek a death sentence. In the first year of the new statute the prosecutor charged first degree murder in only 118 of 468 possible instances (25%). In subsequent analyses we will report those factors that were instrumental in the prosecutor charging a homicide as a first degree murder.

FINDINGS

South Carolina

Table 3.2 reports the results of a maximum likelihood logit analysis[2] where the outcome variable is the decision of the South Carolina prosecutor to seek a sentence of death. There are two models reported in Table 3.2, labeled M1 and M2. In the first model, all exogenous variables are included in the logistic regression equation, while model M2 is a more parsimonious model obtained by stepwise excluding all nonsignificant effects from the full model. It can be seen from Table 3.2 that to a large extent the decision to seek a death sentence in South Carolina is influenced by the prosecutor's consideration of important legal information about each case. What increases the likelihood that the prosecutor will seek the death penalty is the number of statutory aggravating factors, the number of felony offenses committed in addition to murder (rape, armed robbery, kidnapping), the existence of general factors in aggravation (brutality, binding the victim, making the victim plead for his or her life, etc.), the absence of mitigating factors, and the use of torture. It would seem, then, that the local prosecutor in South Carolina makes an assessment of the overall egregiousness of homicide cases and pursues the death penalty only in the most serious of those cases. This would appear to confirm Justice White's expectation in *Gregg* that statutory aggravating and mitigating circumstances which are supposed to guide the discretion of the jury serve a similar function for the prosecutor, bringing rationality and consistency to the capital sentencing process.

Table 3.2 Maximum Likelihood Logit Estimates of Factors Influencing the Decision of the Prosecutor in South Carolina to Seek a Death Sentence

Factor	M1	M2
Number of Victims	−.308	
Number of Offenders	.185	
Type of Weapon	.366	
Victim/Offender Relationship	.235	
Race of Victim	.867*	.898**
Race of Offender	−.269	
Total Number of Aggravating Factors	1.797***	1.688***
Number of Statutory Felony Offenses	1.220**	1.217**
General Factors in Aggravation	1.291**	1.490***
Factors in Mitigation	−.718*	−.744*
Sex of Victim	.680*	
Age of Victim	−.418	
Use of Torture	1.199*	1.225*
Use of a Personal Weapon	−1.146	
Constant	−3.179	−2.295
Likelihood Ratio	154.16	145.56
degrees of freedom	14	6

* p < .05   Model M1 is a full model including all exogenous variables, Model M2 is a reduced model containing
** p < .01   only those significant effects from the first model. In this more parsimonious model, one effect (sex of
*** p < .001   victim) was no longer statistically significant.

Table 3.2 also clearly reveals, however, that legal factors are not the only ones influencing the decision of the South Carolina prosecutor to seek a death sentence. The logistic regression analysis indicates that although the race of the defendant has no significant effect on this decision, the race of the victim is an important consideration. Consistent with other post-*Gregg* research (Bowers & Pierce, 1980; Gross & Mauro, 1984; Baldus et al., 1983), these findings from South Carolina indicate that even after important legal factors of the case are taken into account, South Carolina prosecutors are more likely to seek a death sentence when the victim killed was white rather than black.

Table 3.3 reports a more refined analysis of this racial effect, by considering the combined effect of race of victim and defendant. In these logistic regressions a parsimonious model is estimated which includes only those variables that were already found to be significantly related to the prosecutors charging decision (Table 3.2), and a race variable. The first model (M1) includes a racial dummy variable where those homicides involving a black killing a white (coded 1) are compared with all others. This racial effect is positive and significant, indicating that compared with homicides involving all other racial combinations, prosecutors in South Carolina are significantly more likely to seek a death sentence when a black defendant crosses racial lines and slays a white victim than for all other homicides. This is true even when other legally relevant facts of the case are considered. The second model reported in Table 3.3 (M2) includes a racial dummy variable where intraracial black homicides are compared with homicides involving all other racial combinations. This effect is significant and negative, indicating that even with relevant case characteristics considered, homicides in South Carolina that involve a black slaying another black are significantly less likely to result in the prosecutor seeking the death penalty than in cases involving other racial combinations. Together, these data suggest that the racial effect observed for South Carolina homicides is of two sorts: (1) an inclination for prosecutors to seek a death sentence when a black slays a white, and (2) a disinclination for the same prosecutors to do so when a black slays another black, even for homicides of comparable seriousness.

Table 3.3 Maximum Likelihood Logit Estimates of Factors Influencing the Decision of the Prosecutor in South Carolina to Seek a Death Sentence

Factor	M1	M2
Race #	.768**	−1.067**
Total Number of Aggravating Factors	1.664***	1.697***
Number of Statutory Felony Offenses	1.254***	1.207**
General Factors in Aggravation	1.514***	1.456***
Factors in Mitigation	−.760**	−.787**
Use of Torture	1.302*	1.133*
Constant	−2.620	−2.071
Likelihood Ratio	145.44	146.84
degrees of freedom	6	6

*   p < .05
** p < .01
*** p < .001

#In model M1 the race effect is coded 1 for homicides where a black killed a white and 0 for all others, in model M2 the race effect is coded 0 for homicides where a black killed another black and 1 for all others.

Previous research by Bowers and Pierce (1980) has suggested that the imposition of death sentences may vary by different geographic regions of the state. Our interest in geographic effects here, however, is restricted to the conditional effect that geography may have on the influence of race. It may be that racial considerations are more important in different cultural, political, or judicial climates. Tables 3.4 and 3.5 report the results of two separate logistic regression analyses where the decision of the prosecutor to seek a death sentence is examined within both urban (Table 3.4) and rural (Table 3.5) jurisdictions. Some support for a conditional effect can be found. For example, the finding previously discussed concerning the effect of victim's race seems mainly characteristic of urban jurisdictions in South Carolina. The effect of victim's race is significant in urban counties of the state but not in rural counties. Also, the direction of the effect for the race of the offender is different in urban and rural areas. Urban prosecutors in South Carolina are more inclined to seek the death penalty against white offenders, controlling for the aforementioned legal factors, while rural prosecutors have a slight bias against black defendants. When these two opposite effects were combined in the pooled analysis (Table 3.2), their countervailing effects were canceled out. In addition to these racial differences, a few other explanatory variables have different effects in urban regions of the state than they do in rural areas. For example, while urban prosecutors are more likely to seek a death sentence if the victim was killed by a gun, rural prosecutors are more likely to do so if the victim was killed by strangulation or beaten. In addition, the number of victims had a negative effect on the likelihood of urban prosecutors seeking the death penalty but a positive effect on rural prosecutors. Finally, factors in mitigation had no effect on the decision to seek a death sentence in urban areas of South Carolina but did reduce the probability of a death sentence request in more rural areas of the state.

Table 3.4 Maximum Likelihood Logit Estimates of Factors Influencing the Decision of the Prosecutor in South Carolina to Seek a Death Sentence: Urban Counties

Factor	M1	M2
Number of Victims	−2.896*	−2.400*
Number of Offenders	−.026	
Type of Weapon	2.367**	2.321**
Victim/Offender Relationship	.928	
Race of Victim	1.273	1.844*
Race of Offender	2.325**	1.997**
Total Number of Aggravating Factors	2.712**	2.860***
Number of Statutory Felony Offenses	1.738**	2.402**
General Factors in Aggravation	1.761*	1.985*
Factors in Mitigation	.327	
Sex of Victim	1.223	
Age of Victim	−.221	
Constant	−6.502	−6.036
Likelihood Ratio	73.18	69.70
degrees of freedom	12	7

* $p < .05$
** $p < .01$
*** $p < .001$

Table 3.5 Maximum Likelihood Logit Estimates of Factors Influencing the Decision of the Prosecutor in South Carolina to Seek a Death Sentence: Rural Counties

Factor	M1	M2
Number of Victims	1.503*	1.524*
Number of Offenders	−.107	
Type of Weapon	.006	
Victim/Offender Relationship	.283	
Race of Victim	−.213	
Race of Offender	−.069	
Total Number of Aggravating Factors	1.406**	1.452***
Number of Statutory Felony Offenses	.370	
General Factors in Aggravation	1.785**	1.725**
Factors in Mitigation	−.964*	−.787*
Use of a Personal Weapon	−1.549*	−1.388*
Sex of Victim	.371	
Age of Victim	−.411	
Constant	−1.176	−1.390
Likelihood Ratio	59.60	56.04
degrees of freedom	12	7

* $p < .05$
** $p < .01$
*** $p < .001$

In sum, these data suggest that the decision of the prosecutor in South Carolina to seek a death sentence in a capital murder is in part explained by the characteristics of the homicide (factors in aggravation and mitigation) and in part by race. Contrary to the pre-*Furman* literature which suggested a race of offender bias, this research in South Carolina is consistent with others in different states (Bowers & Pierce, 1980; Baldus et al., 1983; Gross & Mauro, 1984) which indicates the more subtle presence of victim-based racial discrimination. In addition, some preliminary data also suggest that the effect that race has on prosecutors' charging decisions may not be uniform, but may vary with local conditions.

North Carolina

Tables 3.6 and 3.7 report comparable, but somewhat more limited, data on the decision of North Carolina prosecutors to seek a death sentence. The outcome variable in these tables is the decision of the prosecutor to charge an offense as a first degree murder (coded 1) rather than a lesser type (coded 0). Since capital punishment can only be imposed in North Carolina for first degree murder, the decision to charge murder in the first degree is tantamount to a decision to seek the death penalty, and both one of the most important and earliest decisions made in the processing of a murder case.

Table 3.6 reports the estimation of three different logistic regression models. In the first (M1), all North Carolina cases are pooled together, in the second (M2) only urban homicide cases are considered, while model three (M3) separately examines only rural murders. In looking first at model M1, it can be seen that North Carolina prosecutors charge a case as a first degree murder to a large extent based on its overall degree of seriousness. The most significant effect observed here is for the variable called Scale of Aggravation, which is an indicator of the general egregiousness of the homicide. The significant positive effect shows that first degree murder charges are reserved for the most aggravated homicides. In addition to the aggravation of the homicide, first degree murder indictments are significantly more likely for male offenders, if there is strong evidence to suggest that the defendant was culpable for his actions, and for those homicides involving the killing of a single victim.[3] Although not significant, model M1 also suggests that a first degree murder indictment is more likely to be sought if a female rather than a male was killed and if it was a murder committed during the commission of another felony. Contrary to the findings reported for South Carolina, North Carolina prosecutors are not strongly motivated by racial considerations when making their charging decisions. Neither the race of the offender nor the race of the victim was significantly related to this decision.

Table 3.6 Maximum Likelihood Logit Estimates of Factors Influencing the Decision of the Prosecutor in North Carolina to Seek a Death Sentence

Factor	M1	M2	M3
Race of Offender	.043	−.118	.246
Race of Victim	.008	.220	−.149
Sex of Offender	−.590*	−.064	−1.962*
Sex of Victim	.339	.228	.312
Strength of the Evidence	−.042	−.240	−.007
Number of Victims	−1.036*	1.791*	−1.623
Felony-Type Murder	.328	.420	−.166
Scale of Aggravation	.049***	.087***	−.054
Scale of Mitigation	−.003	−.020	.060*
Factors in Self-Defense	−.171	−.100	−.071
Culpability Index	.174*	.105	.364
Constant	−1.309	−1.107	−1.312
Likelihood Ratio	25.51	32.11	13.10
degrees of freedom	11	11	11

* $p < .05$
** $p < .01$
*** $p < .001$

Model M1 includes all homicides, Model M2 includes only those homicides committed in urban areas, Model M3 includes only those homicides committed in rural areas.

The prosecutor's charging decision in North Carolina is modeled separately for urban (M2) and rural (M3) areas in Table 3.6. In urban jurisdictions the decision of the prosecutor is strongly influenced by the overall degree of aggravation present in the homicide. There is also a significant effect observed for the number of victims killed. In urban areas the effect for the number of victims is positive, indicating that a first degree murder indictment is more likely in multiple victim homicides than in those where only a single victim is killed. Race seems to have no significant effect on urban prosecutors' charging decisions. However, even though the effect of victim's race is not statistically significant, prosecutors in urban areas of North Carolina are almost twice (1.65) as likely to charge first degree murder for the slaying of a white than a black. In comparison with urban jurisdictions, modeling the decision of rural North Carolina prosecutors was more difficult. The only significant exogenous variables, and these were only modestly significant, were for the sex of the offender and the presence of mitigating factors (which *slightly increased* the probability of a first degree murder indictment). Neither the race of the victim nor the race of the offender had much of an effect on rural prosecutors. It also should be noted that the model for the rural prosecutors' charging decision had a much worse fit to the data than that for urban prosecutors, suggesting much greater variability in their decision-making.

Table 3.7 reports the results of a final logistic regression analysis. In these two models all prosecutors are pooled together. In the first of these (M1) the race effect is dummy coded where a code of 0 is given to all black-on-black homicides, in the second model the race effect involves a comparison of black-on-white slayings (coded 1) with all others. Neither of these two race variables is significant with legally relevant variables in the model, and the reported effect is substantively negligible. Again, contrary to the case for South Carolina, the likelihood of a death sentence request by the prosecutor is not affected by the racial combination of victim and offender.

Table 3.7 Maximum Likelihood Logit Estimates of Factors Influencing the Decision of the Prosecutor in North Carolina to Seek a Death Sentence

Factor	M1	M2
Race	.052	.010
Sex of Offender	−.587*	−.587*
Sex of Victim	.343	.344
Strength of the Evidence	−.042	−.041
Number of Victims	−1.041*	−1.025*
Felony-Type Murder	.321	.336
Scale of Aggravation	.049**	.048**
Scale of Mitigation	−.003	−.003
Factors in Self-Defense	−.171	−.168
Culpability Index	.173	.172
Constant	−1.312	−1.291
Likelihood Ratio	25.52	25.47
degrees of freedom	11	11

*   p < .05   In Model M1 the race effect is a dummy variable coded 0 for homicides involving a black killing a
**   p < .01   black and 1 for all others, in Model M2 the race effect is dummy coded 1 for homicides where a black
*** p < .001   kills a white and 0 for all others.

CONCLUSIONS

This chapter has examined one decision-making point in the capital sentencing process of two states: the decision of the local prosecutor to seek a sentence of death given the commission of a homicide that is statutorily eligible for the death penalty. In procedurally and substantively reforming state death penalty laws, the United States Supreme Court went to great lengths to ensure that the discretion of capital sentencers would be appropriately guided and structured in order to reduce levels of arbitrariness and discrimination. Perhaps because the Court has typically viewed the power of the prosecutor as essentially an administrative matter, and generally beyond the purview of its own powers of constitutional review, it made no explicit attempt to guide or provide a review of the discretion typically exercised by prosecutors. Or, the Court may have adopted Justice White's position in *Gregg* that sentencing guides would filter down and inform the decision of the prosecutor in determining for which cases a penalty of death will be sought. In any event, neither the capital statutes of North or South Carolina provide any restrictions on the discretion of the prosecutor.

An empirical analysis of capital charging decisions reported in this chapter has suggested that the optimism of the Court may have been misplaced. In both North and South Carolina the decision of the prosecutor to seek a death sentence is influenced by appropriate legal characteristics of the case. In that sense, prosecutorial decision-making can be described as both rational and evenhanded. However, even when these legal considerations were taken into account, the race of the offender and victim (particularly the latter) was influential in deciding which capital defendants would face a capital charge in South Carolina but not in North Carolina. It is not immediately clear why there was strong evidence of victim-based racial discrimination in one state and very little in a contiguous state with a similar legislative scheme. It may be because the North Carolina data only included the first year of death penalty cases, limiting the opportunity for discrimination. It also may be due to the differential effectiveness of the respective models of prosecutorial decision-making. The estimated models for South Carolina's prosecutors demonstrated a much better fit to the data than the North Carolina models. The failure to find stronger evidence of racial discrimination in North Carolina also is somewhat surprising given the consistent effect observed in the literature from other states. Before it can be concluded that North Carolina is an anomaly in that it has eliminated vestiges of racial discrimination from the administration of capital punishment, however, far more detailed research needs to be conducted. It is clear that since the decision of the prosecutor to seek a death sentence occurs early in the capital sentencing process, it is a critical stage in the entire scheme. A stage which under current death penalty jurisprudence is untouched by legal reform. There is a suggestion in this research and that of others that at least some stages in the imposition of capital punishment in the

United States are not fulfilling the promise of *Gregg* that capital justice would be evenhandedly administered.

NOTES

[1] One of the most important differences to be noted is that the North Carolina Statute is similar to Georgia's in having as a statutory aggravating circumstance the commission of a murder that is "especially heinous, atrocious, or cruel" (#9). South Carolina's statute does not contain such a provision, and most of its capital murders are those that involve offenders committing a contemporaneous felony.

[2] A multivariate logit analysis is comparable to an ordinary least squares (OLS) regression. The effect parameters of a logit model reflect the effect of an exogenous variable on the outcome variable once other exogenous variables in the model have been considered. The logit effect indicates the effect of the explanatory variable on the log of the odds of the dependent variable. Logistic regression was chosen in all analyses here since the outcome variable is a dichotomy ("death sentence sought;" "not sought").

[3] It should be noted that this counter-intuitive effect also was found among urban prosecutors in South Carolina (see Table 3.4).

REFERENCES

Baldus, D.C., C. Pulaski & G. Woodworth (1983). "Comparative Review of Death Sentences: An Empirical Study of the Georgia Experience." *Journal of Criminal Law and Criminology,* 74(Fall):661-753.

Bowers, W.J. & G.L. Pierce (1980). "Arbitrariness and Discrimination Under Post-*Furman* Capital Statutes." *Crime and Delinquency,* 26(October):563-575.

Gross, S.R. & R. Mauro (1984). "Patterns of Death: An Analysis of Racial Disparities in Capital Sentencing and Homicide Victimization." *Stanford Law Review,* 37 (November):27-153.

Nakell, B. & K.A. Hardy (1987). *The Arbitrariness of the Death Penalty.* Philadelphia: Temple University Press.

Paternoster, R. (1983). "Race of Victim and Location of Crime: The Decision to Seek the Death Penalty in South Carolina." *Journal of Criminal Law and Criminology,* 74(Fall):754-785.

Paternoster, R. & A.M. Kazyaka (1988). "The Administration of the Death Penalty in South Carolina: Experiences Over the First Few Years." *South Carolina Law Review,* 39(Winter):245-414.

4

Kentucky Prosecutors' Decision to Seek the Death Penalty: A LISREL Model*

Thomas J. Keil
University of Louisville

Gennaro F. Vito
University of Louisville

INTRODUCTION

In the present study, we examine the factors involved in the definition of the seriousness of a homicide and the way in which such a definition influences Kentucky prosecutors' decisions about seeking the death penalty. We are particularly interested in the role, if any, that race plays in prosecutors' evaluations of the seriousness of a murder.

Murder, as a crime, is a social construct, just as are other crimes or acts of social deviance (Becker, 1963; Erikson, 1966; Lemert, 1951; Matza, 1969; Schur, 1971). Murder is an offense defined by the State in and through its criminal laws. Within the federal and state criminal justice systems, certain types of killings are selected out of the universe of killings and are defined as deserving of criminal sanction. At the same time, others are not defined as criminal acts and, hence, are not subject to punishment with criminal sanctions. For example, in many legal jurisdictions in the United States, deaths that result from hazards encountered in the workplace or deaths that result from industrial pollution, or from faulty or poorly designed products, or the like are not punishable as criminal acts. At most, the punishments inflicted on individuals judged to be responsible for such deaths

* Revised version of paper presented at Annual Meetings, American Sociological Association, San Francisco (August, 1989). This paper was developed under a research completion grant from the University of Louisville under the sponsorship of President Donald C. Swain. Points of view expressed in this paper are those of the authors and do not necessarily represent the official position of the University of Louisville or the Commonwealth of Kentucky.

are civil, rather than criminal. Criminal codes not only define what constitutes murder as a criminal act, but they also make distinctions as to the level of seriousness of various types of criminal killings.

In Kentucky, as in many other jurisdictions, murders in which there are more than one victim, murders that involve a concurrent felony, murders of a law enforcement officer, and murders committed by someone with a history of convictions for violent offenses are defined in law as being eligible for prosecution as a capital offense. Prosecutors, however, are not bound to charge a defendant with a capital crime when any one of these circumstances is present. They have the discretionary authority to file lesser charges if they believe the situation warrants. Such prosecutorial discretion opens the door to possible discrimination against minorities or, at the very least, to the introduction of arbitrary and capricious decisions as to who will be prosecuted for a capital crime.

In examining who ends up on death row, social scientists have shown surprisingly little attention to the way in which the criminal justice system responds at various decision-points, so that people are either moved along toward a death sentence or toward some lesser sentence. Among the studies that have examined this aspect of the capital sentencing process are those of Bowers (1983); Nakell and Hardy (1987); Paternoster (1983); Radelet (1981); Radelet and Pierce (1985).

Before 1972, when the Supreme Court's decision in *Furman v. Georgia* (408 U.S. 238) led to subsequent revisions in state death penalty statutes, social scientists generated a substantial body of research evidence suggesting that the capital sentencing process produced outcomes in which blacks were far more likely to receive a death sentence than were whites (Garfinkle, 1949; Johnson, 1957; Johnson, 1941). Research also showed that whites were more likely than blacks to have death sentences commuted to a lesser sentence (Wolfgang, Kelly & Nolde, 1962).

Racial differences in capital sentencing in rape cases also were observed. Wolfgang and Riedel (1973) showed that blacks convicted of raping whites were 18 times more likely to attract a death sentence than were others. Kleck (1981) also found evidence of racial effects in death sentences for rape in the South.

Furman v. Georgia led to a brief hiatus in the imposition of the death penalty in the United States. However, as a result of the Supreme Court's decision in *Gregg v. Georgia* (428 U.S. 153, 1976), states adopted new statutes that met the Supreme Court's requirements for a constitutionally valid imposition of the death penalty. Research since *Gregg,* however, suggests that "guided discretion" may not work in the way that the U.S. Supreme Court hoped it would. Where "guided discretion" laws have been put into effect the research evidence indicates that laws have not ended arbitrary and discriminatory sentencing in capital crimes. For example, studies by Riedel (1976); Zimring, Eigen, and O'Malley (1976); and Lewis (1978) all found that blacks charged with murdering whites were more likely to receive a death sentence than were other race of the offender—race of the victim combinations. Bowers and Pierce (1980) conducted a study of capital sentencing in four states (Florida, Georgia, Ohio, and Texas) and found that blacks convicted of killing whites were more likely to receive a death sentence than were other race-of-the-murderer/race-of-the-victim combinations.

Studies of the capital sentencing process in Florida demonstrate that blacks charged with the murder of whites have a greater risk of receiving a death sentence than do either whites who kill blacks, whites who kill whites, or blacks who kill blacks (Arkin, 1980; Radelet, 1981; Radelet & Pierce, 1985). Also for Florida, Foley and Powell (1982) and Bowers (1983) demonstrated that jurors were more likely to issue, and judges to impose, a death sentence in white victim cases than in cases where the victim was not white.

Other studies have suggested a similar pattern in other states. Paternoster (1983) found that in South Carolina, even after controlling for a number of aggravating and mitigating circumstances, the murder of a white by a black was more likely to result in a capital sentence than the murder of a black by a black. Gross and Mauro (1984) studied the capital sentencing process in eight states (Arkansas, Florida, Georgia, Illinois, Mississippi, North Carolina, Oklahoma, and Virginia) and found that blacks who killed whites were several times more likely to receive a death sentence than were other murderers. More recent research in Louisiana (Smith, 1987) also discovered evidence of discrimination in sentencing for capital crimes by race of the victim.

While the studies of capital punishment cited above all show that race plays a role in the imposition of the death penalty, still other research has failed to find evidence of racial discrimination in the capital sentencing process. With respect to the death sentence, Kleck (1981) has found no evidence of pervasive racial effects on death sentencing practices except for rape. Barnett (1985) has found that race is important only across a limited range of cases classified by their seriousness. For Georgia, Barnett (1985) found racial effects among the cases of intermediate seriousness, while there was little sign of racial bias among murders that were of low and high seriousness. Radelet (1981) has found that race of the offender does not have a significant effect on death sentences, rather, he has shown that race of the victim appears to be more important in determining who is and who is not sentenced to death.

One of the reasons put forward to explain why the older studies found such powerful racial effects in the capital sentencing process is the methodological inadequacy of many of these studies (see, for example, Kleck, 1981 and Barnett, 1985). Critics have noted that one of the major problems with many of the earlier studies is that they often failed to account for a variety of factors that, on theoretical grounds, might be expected to have effects on the criminal justice system's response to homicides. Critics argue that had such factors been included in these studies, racial differences in sentencing either would be substantially reduced or would disappear altogether.

In an attempt to overcome such criticisms, more recent studies (for example, see Baldus, Pulaski & Woodworth, 1985; Paternoster, 1983; Zeisel, 1981) of sentencing differentials have included a variety of factors that were ignored in earlier research. Among the more important of such factors have been various indicators of the seriousness of the homicide, variables pertaining to characteristics of the victim, and variables describing the relationship of the victim to the killer.

Despite the methodological refinements of the more recent studies, Barnett (1985) has advanced an important statistical critique of contemporary capital sentencing studies. His central point is that the multivariate statistical procedures used to partial out the relative contribution of the various factors, including race-related variables, to sentencing outcomes are inadequate to the task at hand. He argues that the high correlations between various indicators of the seriousness of homicides and the correlations between race and various indicators of seriousness preclude determining the relative importance of any given variable by meaningful statistical criteria.

In order to overcome these difficulties, Barnett (1985) suggested an alternative research strategy built around the construction of a scale designed to measure the overall seriousness of a homicide. Barnett (1985:1339) measured the seriousness of the homicide using a classification system that considered the following three dimensions:

1) "The Certainty the Defendant is a Deliberate Killer
2) The 'Status' of the Victim
3) The Heinousness of the Killing."

The first dimension refers to the degree of assurance that the defendant in question was the killer of the victim and that the defendant acted in a knowing manner to cause the victim's death (Barnett, 1985:1339-1340). The second dimension deals with the nature of the relationship between the defendant and the victim (Barnett, 1985:1340). The third dimension considers such questions as whether the killing involved some element of self-defense and/or how "vile" was the homicide (Barnett, 1985:1341). Using this scale, Barnett, as indicated above, went on to show the absence of pervasive racial effects in Georgia's capital sentencing process. In creating this scale and carrying out his analysis, Barnett used data initially collected by Baldus et al. (1983).

Barnett's (1985) work suggests a promising path for research on capital sentencing. However, his attempt to construct an overall scale of seriousness of a homicide is not without its own problems. For example, Barnett treats all of the components of any given dimension of seriousness as having relatively equal weight in determining the score a given case receives on a particular dimension. In addition, he does not allow for the possibility that individual components within any dimension also might be part of another dimension. Finally, Barnett does not specify how the various dimensions are interrelated.

In the present study, our objective is to build on Barnett's (1985) premise that it is preferable to use an overall indicator of seriousness of a crime, rather than a host of individual variables, when attempting to predict the response of any given component of the criminal justice system to the capital sentencing process. Rather than constructing our measure of seriousness purely on *a priori* grounds, we will take a different tack. In addition, we will examine the predictive validity of our unmeasured variable(s) upon prosecutors' reactions to a homicide. In estimating a measurement model and a structural model, we are addressing important issues of construct validity with respect to the concept of "seriousness" of a killing.

DATA AND METHODS

The universe of cases consists of all persons charged, indicted, convicted, and sentenced for murders in Kentucky between December 22, 1976 (the date the most recent Kentucky capital sentencing statute went into effect) and October 1, 1986 (N = 864). Institutional files compiled and maintained by the Kentucky Corrections Cabinet were the main source for data both on offenders and victims. Of the initial 864 cases, 557 met the minimum legal requirements to be tried on capital charges. Of this number, we had complete data for 401 cases. The largest number of cases excluded had missing data on race of the victim and/or race of the killer. In the analyses that follow we focus on the 401 cases for which we had complete data and which met the legal requirements for being charged with a capital offense in Kentucky.

ANALYSES

We conceive of Seriousness (S) as a unidimensional unmeasured, i.e., latent, variable (Joreskog & Sorbom, 1986). The proposed indicators for our latent, exogenous variable are as follows:

1. CONCUR—scored one if the accused had committed a Robbery I; Burglary I; Rape I, Sodomy I; and/or Arson I in conjunction with the homicide and zero if not;
2. MDEATH—scored one if there was more than one victim and zero if there only was one victim;
3. KMAGG—scored one if the accused had more than one of the factors that Kentucky law defines as an aggravating circumstance and zero if only one statutory aggravating circumstance is present;
4. SILENCE—scored one if the accused had killed a victim in order to prevent a victim from giving testimony against the accused and zero if not;

5. BLACK KILLED WHITE (BKW)—scored one if the crime involved the killing of a white by a black and zero if the murder involved a black who killed a black, a white who killed a white, or a white who killed a black;

6. SEX OF VICTIM (SEXV)—scored one if the victim was female and zero if the victim was male;

7. VICTIM-OFFENDER RELATIONSHIP (VOREL)—scored one if the victim was a stranger and zero if the victim was not a stranger to the accused.

8. VIOLENT HISTORY (VHIST)—scored one if the accused had been convicted of a violent offense in the past and zero if the accused had no prior convictions for violent acts.

CONCUR, MDEATH, AND VHIST all are defined in Kentucky law as aggravating circumstances. KMAGG indicates whether more than one aggravating circumstance was present in the homicide. While Kentucky law does not require prosecutors to take into account how many aggravating circumstances might have accompanied a homicide, KMAGG still may be thought of as a legally grounded factor. SEXV, VOREL, and BKW have been included as potential indicators of SERIOUSNESS based upon the fact that they have been found in previous studies, cited above, to be related to one or another steps in the capital sentencing process.

The endogenous variable is a single indicator latent variable, DQJURY. It is scored one if the accused has been charged with a capital crime and zero if the prosecutor has not decided to seek a capital sentence.

For the measurement compontent of the model, our hypothesis is that SERIOUSNESS (S) is a unidimensional construct. We therefore expect that all of the variables will load on just one latent variable, including not only those pertaining to the legal aspects and the objective heinousness of the crime, such as MDEATH, CONCUR, SILENCE, and KMAGG, but also those indicating the sex of the victim (SEXV), the race of the victim and the accused (BKW), the social relationship of the victim and the accused (VOREL), and the indicator of a past conviction of a violent crime (VHIST).

Table 4.1 Frequency Distributions (N = 401)

Variable	Frequency	% Frequency
CONCUR		
No	213	53.1
Yes	188	46.9
MDEATH		
No	345	86.0
Yes	56	14.0
VHIST		
No	139	34.7
Yes	262	65.3
SEX OF VICTIM		
Male	281	70.1
Female	120	29.9
RACE OF OFFENDER—RACE OF VICTIM		
Black Killed Black	75	18.7
Black Killed White	44	11.0
White Killed White	269	67.1
White Killed Black	13	3.2
VICTIM-OFFENDER RELATIONSHIP		
Non-Stranger	287	71.6
Stranger	114	28.4
SILENCE		
No	329	82.0
Yes	72	18.0
KMAGG		
No	246	61.3
Yes	155	38.7
DQJURY		
No	297	74.1
Yes	104	25.9

Table 4.2 Tetrachoric Correlation Coefficients

	CONCUR	MDEATH	SILENCE	BKW	KMAGG	SEXV	VOREL	VHIST	DJ
CONCUR	1.00								
MDEATH	−.06	1.00							
SILENCE	.70	.12	1.00						
BKW	.41	−.22	.15	1.00					
KMAGG	.75	.34	.53	.20	1.00				
SEXV	.10	.01	.20	.07	.10	1.00			
VOREL	.66	−.29	.32	.63	.40	−.07	1.00		
VHIST	−.54	−.43	−.18	−.26	.30	−.09	−.27	1.00	
DQJURY	.52	.35	.53	.35	.53	.21	.21	−.24	1.00

Table 4.1 contains the frequency distributions for the variables used in building our models, as well as other factors of interest. As can be seen in this table, most murders in Kentucky are committed by whites who are killing whites. The second largest category of killings involve blacks who kill blacks. Therefore, it is evident that murder in Kentucky occurs within, rather than across, racial categories.

Table 4.2 contains a matrix of tetrachoric correlations for the variables we use to construct Unweighted Least Squares (ULS) models. Given that Pearson product-moment correlations among dichotomous variables are likely to violate several of the key statistical assumptions in covariance structure models, Joreskog and Sorbom (1986) and Muthen (1984) recommend tetrachoric correlations for dichotomous variables, rather than product-moment correlations, as the basis for estimating models. The tetrachoric correlations, as well as the ULS models, were generated using LISREL VI (Joreskog & Sorbom, 1986). Tetrachoric correlations are special cases of polychoric correlations. Polychoric correlations are correlations between pairs of ordinal variables, each of which is regarded as an approximation of some underlying continuous variable (Joreskog & Sorbom, 1986).

Tables 4.3 and 4.5 present the parameter estimates for our initial model and our final acceptable model, respectively. Table 4.4 presents the Goodness of Fit Index (GFI), the Adjusted Goodness of Fit Index (AGFI), and the Root Mean Square Residual (RMSR) for several models that we developed and tested for various equality constraints on the Lambdas. The GFI measures the "relative amount of variances and covariances accounted for by the model" (Joreskog & Sorbom, 1986:I.41), while the AGFI provides the same measure, adjusting for the degrees of freedom of the model. The magnitude of the GFI is independent of sample size and is "relatively robust against departures from normality" (Joreskog & Sorbom, 1986:I.41). The RMSR measures the "average of the residual variances and covariances" (Joreskog & Sorbom, 1986:I.41).

Our first model involved estimating loadings for all of the possible indicators of "Seriousness." Looking at the parameter estimates presented in Table 4.3, it can be seen that all of the indicators have modest to high loadings on "seriousness." "Seriousness" is the "KSI" in LISREL terminology. It is the technical term for the latent exogenous variable in the LISREL framework. The Goodness of Fit Index (GFI), the Adjusted Goodness of Fit Index (AGFI), and the Root Mean Square Residual (RMSR) indicate that the model has an acceptable degree of fit. In general, a GFI and an AGFI OF .95 or greater is regarded as "acceptable" (see Joreskog & Sorbom, 1986, for a technical discussion of these criteria).

Given these results, we next examined the question of whether the indicator for black killed white could be eliminated as an indicator of the Seriousness construct. We set the parameter estimate for black killed white (BKW) to zero, while allowing the remaining parameters to be unconstrained. As can be seen in Table 4.4, Model 2, as indicated by the AGFI, does not fit the observed data. The AGFI is substantially below the cutoff point of .95, meaning that BKW must be included in the measurement model as an indicator of the seriousness of a homicide.

In Model 3, we allowed BKW to be a free, unconstrained parameter, but set the values of CONCUR and KMAGG equal. This hypothesis is suggested in the results for our first model, which shows that the parameter estimates for these two indicators are very close. Our results indicate that for all intents and purposes the loadings of CONCUR and KMAGG may be regarded as being equal to each other. This indicates that the presence of a concurrent felony is as important as the presence of multiple aggravating circumstances as an indicator of the seriousness of a homicide in Kentucky.

Our next model, Model 4, involved setting the parameter for SILENCE equal to those for KMAGG and CONCUR. Our results, as indicated in Table 4.4, show that we do not lose fit by treating these three variables as having equal loadings on our latent variable.

For Model 5, Lambdas for CONCUR, KMAGG, and SILENCE were set equal. In addition, the Lambdas for BKW and MDEATH were set equal to each other. However, the Lambdas for BKW and MDEATH were not set equal to those for CONCUR, KMAGG, and SILENCE. The results for this model indicate an acceptable level of fit. This is a substantively important model in that it shows that BKW is as important an indicator of the seriousness of a homicide as is one of the legal factors that defines eligibility for a death sentence, i.e., having more than one victim.

In Model 6, Lambdas for CONCUR, KMAGG, and SILENCE were set equal to each other and the Lambdas for BKW and MDEATH were set equal to each other. In addition, we set the Lambda for VOREL equal to that of BKW and MDEATH. This model continues to provide a good fit with the observed correlations, indicating that VOREL'S Lambda can be treated as equal to those of BKW

Table 4.3 Model 1: ULS for DQJURY

	LAMBDA X
CONCUR	.811
MDEATH	.452
SILENCE	.844
BKW	.525
KMAGG	.827
SEXV	.174
VOREL	.426
VHIST	−.471

	GAMMA
ETA	.636

	PSI ETA
ETA	.595

THETA DELTA: ULS

	CONCUR	MDEATH	SILENCE	BKW	KMAGG	SEXV	VOREL	VHIST
CONCUR	.342							
MDEATH	−.426	.796						
SILENCE	.000	−.262	.287					
BKW	.000	−.457	−.293	.725				
KMAGG	.079	.000	−.168	−.334	.316			
SEXV	.000	.000	.000	.000	.000	.970		
VOREL	.315	−.482	.000	.407	.000	−.144	.819	
VHIST	−.158	−.217	.217	.000	.689	.000	.000	.779

SQUARED MULTIPLE CORRELATIONS FOR X VARIABLES

	CONCUR	MDEATH	SILENCE	BKW	KMAGG	SEXV	VOREL	VHIST
Model: ULS	.658	.204	.713	.275	.684	.030	.181	.221

SQUARED MULTIPLE CORRELATIONS FOR STRUCTURAL EQUATIONS

Model 1: = .405

MEASURES OF GOODNESS OF FIT

Goodness of Fit Index (GFI)	.995
Adj. Goodness of Fit Index (AGFI)	.983
Root Mean Square Residual (RMSR)	.031

Table 4.4: ULS Models Estimated: Tetrachoric Correlations

MODEL	GFI	AGFI	RMSR
Model 1	.995	.983	.031
Model 2	.957	.852	.095
Model 3	.995	.984	.031
Model 4	.995	.985	.031
Model 5	.995	.985	.032
Model 6	.995	.985	.033
Model 7	.980	.948	.064

Table 4.5 Model 6: ULS

	LAMBDA X
CONCUR	.826
MDEATH	.462
SILENCE	.826
BKW	.462
KMAGG	.826
SEXV	.175
VOREL	.462
VHIST	−.479

	GAMMA
ETA	.637

	PSI ETA
ETA	.594

THETA DELTA: MODEL 6

	CONCUR	MDEATH	SILENCE	BKW	KMAGG	SEXV	VOREL	VHIST
CONCUR	.318							
MDEATH	−.441	.787						
SILENCE	.000	−.261	.318					
BKW	.000	−.433	−.231	.787				
KMAGG	.068	.000	−.152	−.281	.318			
SEXV	.000	.000	.000	.000	.000	.969		
VOREL	.279	−.503	.000	.417	.000	−.151	.787	
VHIST	−.144	−.209	.216	.000	.696	.000	.000	.771

SQUARED MULTIPLE CORRELATIONS FOR X VARIABLES

	CONCUR	MDEATH	SILENCE	BKW	KMAGG	SEXV	VOREL	VHIST
Model 6: ULS	.682	.213	.682	.213	.682	.031	.213	.229

SQUARED MULTIPLE CORRELATIONS FOR STRUCTURAL EQUATIONS

Model 6 = .406

MEASURES OF GOODNESS OF FIT

Goodness of Fit Index (GFI)	.995
Adj. Goodness of Fit Index (AGFI)	.985
Root Mean Square Residual (RMSR)	.033

and MDEATH. In Kentucky, killing a stranger is as strong an indicator of having committed a serious homicide as is a murder with multiple victims or a murder in which a black has killed a white.

In Model 7, we set the parameter estimate for SEXV equal to those of BKW, MDEATH, and VOREL. In addition, the equality constraint for CONCUR, KMAGG, and SILENCE was retained. The AGFI fell just short of our level of acceptability of .95, indicating that it is not advisable to treat the parameter for SEXV as being equal to those for BKW, MDEATH, and VOREL.

With respect to the measurement component of our final best fitting model (see Table 4.5), Model 6, CONCUR, KMAGG, and SILENCE have the largest positive loadings for our latent variable, SERIOUSNESS. More serious homicides involve a concurrent felony, the presence of more than one legally defined aggravating circumstance, and/or an attempt to prevent the victim from testifying against the accused.

They are followed by the Lambdas for MDEATH, BKW, and VOREL. These effects suggest that where a homicide has multiple victims, where an accused kills a stranger, and/or where a black kills a white the homicide will be taken to be more serious.

SEXV has the smallest positive loading. Killings involving female victims are slightly more likely, compared to those in which the victim is a male, to be taken to be serious killings.

VHIST has a relatively large negative Lambda. This result suggests that it is not the homicide offender with a previous conviction for a violent offense who is defined as having committed the most serious killing. However, there are sizeable positive correlations between the residual of VHIST and KMAGG and VHIST and SILENCE. A more precise specification of these interrelations is necessary in order to account for the negative relationship we have observed.

The final model, as well as its previous iterations, exhibits a number of inter-correlations among the residuals of the various indicators. This suggests that there are additional factors lying outside of our equation that need to be taken into account in future attempts to specify a measurement model for Seriousness.

It also is important to note, with respect to the measurement model, that SERIOUSNESS does not appear to be a multidimensional latent variable. All of the indicators defined by law, as well as the indicators of the social character of the homicide, load on the same KSI, demonstrating that the definition of seriousness that is being used by Kentucky prosecutors is a judgment that blends both legal and extra-legal factors.

Given the loading for VOREL, our results suggest that Barnett (1985) may not have been correct in treating the murder of strangers as a separate dimension of seriousness. Rather, it appears to be but one indicator of a single underlying dimension of the overall seriousness of a killing.

A valid measure of S (Seriousness) should be able to provide a good prediction of our endogenous variable, DQJURY, which indicates whether a homicide offender was or was not charged with a capital crime. Our results indicate that our latent variable, Seriousness (S), has a relatively large effect on DQJURY, which is coded one if the prosecutor tried the defendant before a death-qualified jury and zero if the defendant was not tried before a death-qualified jury. As shown in Table 4.5, the standardized structural coefficient, Gamma, is .637 and the R Squared for the structural equation is .406, indicating that we are explaining greater than 40 percent of the variation in our dependent variable.

DISCUSSION AND CONCLUSION

The analyses demonstrate that LISREL can be used to construct a latent variable to measure the SERIOUSNESS of Kentucky homicides. The results also indicate that the aspects of the homicide defined by Kentucky statute have high loadings on SERIOUSNESS (S). Yet, extra-legal factors, especially VOREL, indicating whether the victim was a stranger to the accused, and BKW, indicating whether a black was charged with the killing of a white, also weigh heavily in the calculation of seriousness. When victims are strangers to the accused or when victims are whites who have been killed by blacks, prosecutors are more apt to charge a defendant with a capital crime, assuming, of course, that they meet the minimum legal requirements for such a charge. This also is the case, though to a lesser degree, when the victim is a woman.

These patterns suggest that prosecutors, while responding to legal aspects of a homicide case, work from a calculus which also includes extra-legal, social factors. Furthermore, at least two social factors, BKW and VOREL, have an influence on the determination of SERIOUSNESS that is equal to at least one of the legal factors, MDEATH. Therefore, race is inextricably bound up with the capital sentencing process in Kentucky. It is a component of SERIOUSNESS and SERIOUSNESS, in turn, has a direct positive effect on prosecutors' decisions.

At this point, we can only speculate as to why the composite of race of the accused-race of the victim is related to SERIOUSNESS of homicides in Kentucky. It may be that Kentucky prosecutors see the murder of whites by blacks as an objectively more heinous killing. On the other hand, the finding may reflect social and political pressures on prosecutors. The public, the media, and other local forces may put pressure on prosecutors to treat such a homicide as an especially serious crime, independent of the other characteristics of the murder, provided that the legal minimum is present for a capital charge. It also is possible that prosecutors treat the murder of a white by a black as a more serious homicide than others for practical, strategic reasons. Prosecutors may believe that it is easier to secure convictions and, therefore, establish a record of successful prosecutions in these types of cases than in others.

It also may be the case that the effects we have observed are the result of factors that we have not included in our model. Such factors might be the location of the homicide, that is, whether it was committed in an urban or a rural area, whether the county in which the homicide took place had a full-time or part-time prosecutor, the strength of the evidence against the accused, or some other factors that we have not identified.

Nevertheless, our efforts demonstrate that it is possible to measure SERIOUSNESS as a latent variable and to estimate the effects of the latent variable on prosecutors' decisions as to whether to seek the death penalty for an accused killer. Conceiving seriousness in this way helps to resolve some of the shortcomings of a single indicator or an indicator-by-indicator approach to estimating the effects of interrelated variables (Barnett, 1985; Pedhazur, 1982).

When a killing meets the minimum legal requirements for a death penalty, our results show that Kentucky prosecutors use extra-legal factors (the social relationship between the victim and the accused, and the race of the accused-race of the victim, and, to a lesser degree, the sex of the victim) to assess a homicide's seriousness. In other words, it is as part of a judgment of SERIOUSNESS that black murderers of whites come to be prosecuted on capital charges to a greater degree than do other homicides involving a different combination of race of the accused-race of the victim in Kentucky.

The integration of BKW murders as a component of SERIOUSNESS suggests that in the post-*Gregg* era, prosecutorial discretion has not been sufficiently curbed in Kentucky so that blacks who kill whites face an equal risk to other killers of being charged with a capital offense. A variety of factors might explain why prosecutors respond the way they do to such homicides. Their response to the murder of whites by blacks may express their personal racial attitudes, it may be a result of external political pressures, it may be a product of political opportunism on the part of prosecutors in that they see these cases as easier to win, or it may result from systemic effects within the decision-making process of the criminal justice system. We do not have data to test these various explanations. But, regardless of which explanation is more accurate, the fact remains that Kentucky's prosecutors define the killing of a white by a black as an especially serious murder. Because of this, blacks who kill whites face a greater risk than others of being charged with a capital crime.

While those black men who have been charged with killing a white bear the brunt of the burden created by Kentucky prosecutors' introduction of racial considerations into the evaluation of the seriousness of a homicide, the inclusion of race as a factor in decisions as to whether to define a killing as a capital crime has far more general consequences for both blacks and whites in American society. First of all, by defining the murder of a white by a black as the type of killing most deserving of capital punishment, prosecutors help to create or at least maintain an illusion among whites that this is THE major form which killing takes as a social problem, despite the fact that, as was shown in Table 4.1, it is far less frequent of a behavior than is the murder of a white by a white or a black by a black.

Second, prosecutors' decisions to use race as an evaluative criterion in defining the seriousness of a murder is but one of many ways in which the State is actively involved in building and maintaining racial boundaries in American society. By defining the murder of a white by a black as an especially serious homicide, prosecutors help to create and maintain white stereotypes of the black community as the repository of an evil subclass that is ready to prey upon whites whenever it has the opportunity to do so. At the same time, prosecutors' behavior contributes to whites' perceptions of their own social world as "normal" and non-pathological. In all likelihood, belief in such a stereotype increases racial fears and the desire to maintain high levels of social distance between blacks and whites. Whites who believe such a stereotype not only will try to avoid casual social relationships with blacks, but whites also will be less supportive of government programs to alleviate the real problems of the black community and more supportive of direct and indirect attempts to suppress the black community.

The measurement model we have developed needs to be tested in other states to see if it holds generally. In addition, other latent variables need to be constructed to take into account other factors which might possibly influence a prosecutor's decision to charge an offender with a capital crime. Among the more important of such factors, and one for which we do not have data, is strength of the evidence (Nakell & Hardy, 1987). Nakell and Hardy found that strength of the evidence influenced decisions at most stages of the capital sentencing process in North Carolina. At the same time, they also found that including strength of the evidence in their log-linear equations did not result in the elimination of racial effects.

REFERENCES

Arkin, S.D. (1980). "Discrimination and Arbitrariness in Capital Punishment: An Analysis of post-*Furman* Murder Cases in Dade County, Florida, 1973-1976." *Stanford Law Review,* 33:75-101.

Baldus, D.C., C. Pulaski & G. Woodworth (1983). "Comparative Review of Death Sentences: An Empirical Study of the Georgia Experience." *Journal of Criminal Law and Criminology,* 74:661-753.

Barnett, A. (1985). "Some Distribution Patterns for the Georgia Death Sentence." *U.C. Davis Law Review,* 18:1327-1374.

Bedau, H.A. (1987). *Death is Different.* Boston: Northeastern University Press.

Becker, H. (1963). *Outsiders.* New York: The Free Press.

Bowers, W.J. (1983). "The Pervasiveness of Arbitrariness and Discrimination Under post-*Furman* Capital Status." *Journal of Criminal Law and Criminology,* 74:1067-1100.

Bowers, W.J. & G.L. Pierce (1980). "Arbitrariness and Discrimination Under post-*Furman* Capital Statutes." *Crime and Delinquency,* 74:1067-1100.

Erikson, K.T. (1966). *Wayward Puritans.* New York: Wiley.

Foley, L.A. & R.S. Powell (1982). "The Discretion of Prosecutors, Judges, and Jurists in Capital Cases." *Criminal Justice Review,* 7:16-22.

Garfinkle, H. (1949). "Research Note on Inter- and Intra-Racial Homicides." *Social Forces,* 27:369-381.

Gross, S.R. & R. Mauro (1984). "Patterns of Death: An Analysis of Racial Disparities in Capital Sentencing and Homicide Victimization." *Stanford Law Review,* 37:27-153.

Johnson, E.H. (1957). Selective Forces in Capital Punishment. *Social Forces,* 36:165-169.

Johnson, G.B. (1941). "The Negro and Crime." *The Annals of the American Academy of Political and Social Science,* 217:93-104.

Joreskog, K.G. & D. Sorbom (1986). *LISREL: Analysis of Linear Structural Relationships by the Method of Maximum Likelihood, Version VI.* Mooresville, IN: Scientific Software, Inc.

Kleck, G. (1981). "Racial Discrimination in Criminal 'Sentencing.'" *American Sociological Review,* 46:783-804.

Legislative Research Commission (1985). *Capital Punishment.* Frankfort, KY: Research Report No. 218.

Lemert, E. (1951). *Social Pathology.* New York: McGraw-Hill.

Lewis, P.W. (1978). "Life on Death Row: A post-*Furman* Profile of Florida's Condemned." In P.W. Lewis & K.D. Peoples (eds.) *The Supreme Court and the Criminal Process—Cases and Comments,* pp. 939-951. Philadelphia: W.B. Saunders.

Matza, D. (1969). *Becoming Deviant.* Englewood Cliffs, NJ: Prentice-Hall.

Muthen, B. (1984). "A General Structural Equation Model with Dichotomous, Ordered Categorical, and Continuous Latent Variable Indicators." *Psychometrica,* 49:115-132.

Nakell, B. & K.A. Hardy (1987). *The Arbitrariness of the Death Penalty.* Philadelphia: Temple University Press.

Paternoster, R. (1983). "Race of the Victim and Location of Crime: The Decision to Seek the Death Penalty in South Carolina." *Journal of Criminal Law and Criminology,* 74:754-785.

Pedhazur, E.J. (1982). *Multiple Regression in Behavioral Research.* Second Edition. New York: Holt, Rinehart, and Winston.

Radelet, M.L. (1981). "Racial Characteristics and the Imposition of the Death Penalty." *American Sociological Review,* 46:918-927.

Radelet, M.L. & G.L. Pierce (1985). "Race and Prosecutorial Discretion in Homicide Cases." *Law and Society Review,* 19:587-621.

Riedel, M. (1976). "Discrimination in the Imposition of the Death Penalty: A Comparison of the Characteristics of Offenders Sentenced pre-*Furman* and post-*Furman.*" *Temple Law Quarterly,* 49:261-283.

Schur, E.M. (1971). *Labeling Deviant Behavior: Its Sociological Implications.* New York: Harper and Row.

Smith, M.D. (1987). "Patterns of Discrimination in Assessments of the Death Penalty: The Case of Louisiana." *Journal of Criminal Justice,* 15:279-286.

Wolfgang, M.E., A. Kelly & H.C. Nodle (1962). "Comparisons of the Executed and the Commuted Among Admissions to Death Row." *Journal of Criminal Law and Criminology,* 53:301-310.

Wolfgang, M.E. & M. Riedel (1973). "Race, Judicial Discretion, and the Death Penalty." *The Annals of the American Academy of Political and Social Science,* 407:119-133.

Zeisel, H. (1981). "Race Bias in the Administration of the Death Penalty: The Florida Experience." *Harvard Law Review,* 95:456-468.

Zimring, F.E., J. Eigen & S. O'Malley (1976). "Punishing Homicides in Philadelphia: Perspectives on the Death Penalty." *University of Chicago Law Review,* 43:227-252.

5

Psychological Testimony and the Decisions of Prospective Death-Qualified Jurors

Frank P. Williams III
Department of Criminal Justice
California State University—San Bernardino

Marilyn D. McShane
Department of Criminal Justice
California State University—San Bernardino

INTRODUCTION

The future dangerousness of a defendant is one of the standard criteria used by many states in the determination of whether capital punishment is an appropriate sentence. Psychiatric testimony from an expert witness is often used to make such a prediction. The United States Supreme Court considers this portion of sentencing so serious that it is said to represent "a life or death matter" (*Satterwhite v. Texas,* 108 S. Ct. 1792, 1988, at 1802).

In a recent decision the Court acknowledged that psychiatric testimony on the future risk of a defendant is "clothed with a scientific authority that often carries great weight with lay juries" (*Satterwhite v. Texas,* at 1801). In the case, a Dr. Grigson, a notorious dangerousness predictor for the state in capital cases, testified that the defendant's sociopathic qualities were not linked to a disease or illness but were, instead, part of his personality. The defendant, Satterwhite, was interviewed after his indictment and arraignment at a time when his Sixth Amendment right to counsel had come into play. At this point the Court also reasoned that the prosecutor had the responsibility of notifying the defense that the results of psychiatric interviews would be used to determine future dangerousness as well as sanity and competence to stand trial.

71

The Supreme Court found that the lack of adequate notice as to the full purpose of the interviews as established in *Estelle v. Smith* (451 U.S. 454, 1981) did not constitute a harmless error as the Texas Court of Criminal Appeals had decided. The justices reversed the appeals decision, ruling that the state had not met the burden of showing beyond a reasonable doubt that testimony of Dr. Grigson had not influenced the jury in sentencing. Justice Marshall wrote that "divining the effect of psychiatric testimony on a sentencer's determination whether death is an appropriate sentence is thus more in the province of soothsayer than appellate judges" (*Satterwhite v. Texas,* at 1802).

The general issues raised in *Satterwhite* are worth examining in the context of the susceptibility of prospective jurors to psychiatric testimony. In this chapter, we do not play soothsayer, but rather assess the attitudes of those who would make up the venire for a capital trial and react to psychiatric testimony. We also estimate the effect of attitudes on pretrial tendencies to convict and sentence.

REVIEW OF PREVIOUS RESEARCH

The way in which personal attitudes and dispositions affect juror decision-making, particularly in capital cases, has been the object of considerable study. In death penalty trials prospective jurors are questioned about their beliefs on capital punishment. Those who are opposed to capital punishment to the extent that their feelings might interfere with their ability to impose a death sentence are excluded from service. These jurors are referred to as death-penalty excludables. On the other hand, all jurors willing to consider the death penalty as a sentencing option are eligible to serve and are referred to as death-qualified jurors.

Research indicates that death-qualified jurors may be more conviction-prone than death-excludable jurors (Bronson, 1970; Cowan, Thompson & Ellsworth, 1984; Goldberg, 1970; Jurow, 1971). The tendency of death-qualified jurors to convict more than excludable jurors is often linked to individual characteristics such as authoritarianism (Boehm, 1968; Goldberg, 1970; Jurow, 1971; Middendorf & Luginbuhl, 1981; Moran & Comfort, 1986), stronger beliefs in just deserts or crime control (Lerner, 1980; Rubin & Peplau, 1975), and less concern about due process (Fitzgerald & Ellsworth, 1984; Luginbuhl & Crocker, 1983).

Luginbuhl and Middendorf (1988) found that death-penalty excludables were more receptive to mitigating circumstances (such as mental illness) and less receptive to aggravating circumstances than death-qualified jurors. Their findings were similar to those of Thompson, Cowan, Ellsworth and Harrington (1984) who concluded that death-qualified jurors tend to favor the prosecution rather than the defense in their approach to a case. This research suggests that defendants, regardless of the merits of the case, are at a disadvantage in capital trials because of death-qualified jurors.

Along with the death-qualified juror's predisposition to favor the prosecution, the defense counsel is disadvantaged by the awareness that a majority of the public mistrusts the insanity defense. In a number of surveys, a significant proportion of the public has consistently expressed the opinion that the plea of insanity is a loophole that allows too many guilty persons to go free (Bronson, 1970; Fitzgerald & Ellsworth, 1984; Harris, 1971).

In a case study using a simulation specifically dealing with insanity pleas, but not necessarily in capital cases, Roberts, Golding and Fincham (1987) found that a serious mental illness (schizophrenia, rather than a less severe personality disorder) was more likely to result in an affirmative finding of insanity, as were acts performed without intent. They also found that bizarre acts increased the likelihood of a guilty but mentally ill finding over a simple guilty verdict.

In an earlier study, Simon (1967) tested participants on psychiatric behavior interpretations and levels of sympathy toward the mentally ill. She found no indication that these measures correlated with subsequent verdicts. However, Ellsworth, Bukaty, Cowan and Thompson (1984) pointed out that Simon was measuring general attitudes toward the mentally ill, and not attitudes toward mentally ill defendants and the insanity defense, which they claim are better predictors of verdicts. In the Ellsworth et al. study, death-qualified jurors believed that only 31 percent of the defendants who pled insanity were really insane, while death-penalty excludables believed that a much higher 56 percent were insane. Ellsworth et al. also found a 30 percent difference between the conviction tendency of death-qualified jurors and death-penalty excludables in two simulated cases of schizophrenic defendants. Using a death-penalty trial scenario, the researchers determined that between 80 to 90 percent of the death-qualified subjects rejected the insanity defense for the two cases.

THE RESEARCH QUESTIONS

Two general issues are critical in estimating the effect of psychiatric testimony in capital cases. First is the issue of credibility and, second, the likelihood that such testimony will change a juror's conviction or sentencing decision. In examining the first issue, three questions are addressed: (1) What level of trust is ascribed to psychiatrists and psychologists by prospective jurors in a capital trial? (2) Does the level of trust ascribed to psychologists and psychiatrists by prospective jurors vary according to whether a juror is death-penalty excludable or death-qualified? (3) Do trust levels vary from those ascribed to other courtroom actors by the two prospective juror groups?

The issue of whether psychiatric testimony changes conviction decisions is more complex. Not only does it require an analysis of the effect of psychiatric testimony on prospective jurors' conviction and sentencing decisions, but there is also the problem of potential interaction between the characteristics of the defendant and the decisions of jurors. Thus, the questions addressed here are: (4) Does information on the defendant's mental condition at the time of the offense affect either the conviction or sentencing decisions of prospective jurors? (5) Is there a difference between the conviction decisions of prospective death-qualified and death-excluded jurors once psychiatric information is proffered? (6) Does psychiatric information interact with the defendant's characteristics in the conviction or sentencing decisions of prospective death-qualified jurors?

METHODOLOGY

The Sample

The data were derived from a mailed survey that contained a completely randomized, multifactor, factorial scenario. Of an initial simple random sample of 10,000 holders of Texas driver's licenses, we drew a second random sample of 2,000 individuals who received the survey instrument. The sample was mailed an introductory letter and, one week later, a questionnaire package with a cover letter, a return envelope and a 12-page questionnaire on jury and trial issues. Those who did not respond within two weeks received a follow-up letter and, if there was still no response, a second questionnaire package was mailed a week later. A fifth and final letter was mailed to those who had not responded within 10 days of the mailing date of the second questionnaire. The survey procedure resulted in 1,389 usable responses, 3 deceased individuals, and 73 letters returned by the post office as nonforwardable for an unadjusted return rate of 69.5 percent. An adjusted return rate of 72 percent was achieved by subtracting both deceased and nonforwardables from the original sample.

The Factorial Scenario

The survey instrument provided a scenario (or vignette) of a capital murder case in which two females were shot, one fatally, during a robbery (see Appendix A). The only personal characteristic used to identify the victims was that they were female. Offender attributes of age (22 and 65 years of age), gender (male and female) and race (white, black, and Hispanic) were randomly interchanged. This resulted in 12 unique offender combinations which were then randomly distributed among the survey subjects. Our research design differs from the factorial surveys developed by Rossi (Rossi & Nock, 1982) in that each respondent received only one of the combinations from the factorial object universe. In other words, ours was not a repeated-measures design. While our design may suffer from some forms of increased measurement error, there is no intra-rater serial correlation or testing threat to internal validity as in the repeated design versions (Cook & Campbell, 1979).

Jury Eligibility

The problem of locating individuals eligible for jury duty was approached from two perspectives. First, we wanted a group of individuals who would be on the jury service list in their hometowns. This was accomplished by asking questions about voter registration and property ownership, the two common jury pool lists used in Texas. People who responded affirmatively to either question were placed in our jury-eligible group. To this group we added a few respondents who reported being summoned for jury duty even though they had neither registered to vote nor owned local real estate. The final jury-eligible group totaled 1,096 persons.

Second, we wanted a group of individuals who would not necessarily be excluded from juries in capital cases. From the general jury-eligible group, we first excluded those who responded that they were opposed to capital punishment. Of the remainder, we further excluded those who answered "yes" to both commonly-worded versions of the *Witherspoon* (391 U.S. 510, 1968) questions ("Would any opposition to the death penalty prevent you: (1) from fairly determining a defendant's guilt or innocence; and (2) from considering death as a possible sentence?"). In this way, we derived the pool of death-penalty excludable jurors. The pool was further reduced by removing all those (32) who answered "yes" to the first *Witherspoon* question, since they would be considered nullifiers (individuals who would not follow the law and instructions of the court). The final group of death-penalty excludables, also known as the guilt-phase includables, numbered 209 respondents.

Finally, any defense attorney would likely challenge the presence of those who would, under any circumstances, automatically sentence a defendant to death in a capital case (*Hovey v. California,* 28 Cal. 3d 1, 616 P.2d 1301, 168 Cal. Rptr. 128, 1980). These automatic-death-penalty (ADP) jurors were excluded by removing those people (86) who responded "always" to the question: "How frequently do you think the death penalty should be used in capital cases?" We cross-validated these responses by making sure that the ADPs also chose the death sentence in response to the factorial scenario. Death-penalty qualified (DPQ) jurors, then, totaled 769 individuals, leaving 209 death-penalty excluded (DPE) jurors, 32 nullifiers, and 86 ADP-excluded jurors.

The Independent Variables

Two independent variables were used. The first was derived from a closed-ended question that followed the conviction and sentencing decisions in the factorial scenario. The question read: "In this case, what would you do if a psychiatrist testified that the person was temporarily insane at the time of the murder?" The respondent was then asked about his or her decision to convict and if the sentence would be changed.[1] Thus, the first independent variable (psychiatric testimony) was based on the concept of "temporary insanity."

A second question asked: "If you were on a jury that found someone guilty of murder, would any of the following conditions of the defendant make you consider a lesser sentence?" A list of conditions following that question included "mentally ill at the time of the murder."[2] Thus, the second independent variable was more general than the first and replaced the term "insanity" with "mental illness."

The Dependent Variables

Three dependent variables—trust, conviction, and sentencing—were used. The first dependent variable was the amount of trust placed in the trial testimony of psychiatrists and psychologists. This concept was measured by asking respondents the following question:

> The media (TV, newspapers, radio) give a picture of court cases as a struggle between opposing sides. Thinking about court cases in general, how do you feel about the "TRUST" you can place in each of these individuals during a trial? Please rate on a scale of 0 to 10 and place an "X" below the number of your choice.

The zero category was defined as "would not trust at all" and the 10 category was defined as "would trust completely." Respondents were then given separate rating scales for various courtroom actors, including a psychologist and a psychiatrist. While this approach could not detect the attitudes of a juror in an actual trial, it was capable of measuring attitudes that prospective jurors bring with them to a voir dire. Further, because the scores were measured at a metric ordinal level, we were able to use a robust parametric statistic (t-test) in the analysis.

The conviction and sentencing dependent variables were categorical. The conviction variable following the scenario contained three response categories: "guilty," "undecided"/"not sure," and "not guilty." Because we intentionally constructed the scenario to include sufficient evidence for conviction, there were very few cases in the "not guilty" category, with over 99 percent of the respondents marking either the "guilty" or "undecided" categories. The conviction variable following the introduction of psychiatric testimony on temporary insanity added the category of "not guilty due to insanity." Both sentencing variables gave respondents a choice of the death penalty, life in prison, a prison sentence, a jail sentence, or a probated sentence.

ANALYSIS

Question 1: *What level of trust is ascribed to psychiatrists and psychologists by prospective jurors in a capital trial?*

The level of trust ascribed to both psychologists and psychiatrists by prospective jurors was slightly over the mid-point of the scale, between "would not trust at all" and "would trust completely" (see Table 5.1). Since a mid-scale score indicates uncertainty, the most reasonable interpretation is that prospective jurors attributed cautious trust to the trial testimony of psychiatrists and psychologists. The difference between trust levels ascribed to psychiatrists and psychologists was not statistically significant.

Table 5.1 Prospective Juror Ratings of Trust Placed in Courtroom Actors

COURT ACTOR	JUROR GROUP	MEAN TRUST	t-VALUE	SD	p
Psychologist	DPQ	5.47	−2.74	2.56	.008
	DPE	6.01		2.44	
Psychiatrist	DPQ	5.53	−2.27	2.55	.023
	DPE	5.98		2.45	
Judge	DPQ	7.54	1.85	2.11	.065
	DPE	7.33		2.22	
Prosecutor	DPQ	5.79	4.53	2.18	.000
	DPE	4.99		2.34	
Police Officer	DPQ	6.36	4.08	2.37	.000
	DPE	5.60		2.48	
Prosecution Witness	DPQ	5.97	2.85	1.92	.004
	DPE	5.53		2.01	
Defense Attorney	DPQ	4.82	−1.28	2.27	.200
	DPE	5.05		2.22	
Defense Witness	DPQ	5.37	.68	1.88	.496
	DPE	5.27		2.14	
Defendant	DPQ	4.43	.65	2.07	.514
	DPE	4.33		2.18	

Question 2: *Does the level of trust ascribed to psychologists and psychiatrists by prospective jurors vary by whether those jurors are death-qualified or death-excluded?*

We calculated the mean response of both DPQ and DPE jurors to the amount of trust they would place in the testimony of both a psychologist and a psychiatrist (see Table 5.1). In both cases the DPE group exhibited a higher level of trust. A t-test of the significance of the difference between the means of the two groups yielded a significant result for both psychologists (t = −2.74, p = .008) and psychiatrists (t = −2.27, p = .023). The DPQ group was less likely to trust the trial testimony of psychiatrists and psychologists.

Question 3: *Do these trust levels vary from those ascribed to other courtroom actors by the two groups?*

The reported levels of trust placed in other courtroom actors did, in fact, differ from those of psychiatrists and psychologists (see Table 5.1). The trust levels for psychiatrists and psychologists were the *only* instances of the DPQs scoring significantly lower than the DPEs. In comparison to the DPEs, the DPQs were significantly more trusting of prosecutors, police officers, and prosecution witnesses. Also, relative to the other categories, DPQs reported trust levels lower than those ascribed to psychiatrists and psychologists only for defense witnesses, defense attorneys and the defendant. These results suggest that the "pretrial" credibility of testimony by mental health professionals may not be particularly high. Further, the removal of DPEs from the guilt phase of a trial would serve to decrease the level of that credibility since they attributed higher levels of trust than did the DPQs.

Question 4: *Does psychiatric testimony on the defendant's mental condition at the time of the offense affect either the conviction or sentencing decisions of prospective jurors?*

The effect of a mental condition on conviction decisions was examined by asking prospective jurors if the original conviction decision they made, based on the scenario, would change if a psychiatrist testified that the defendant was temporarily insane at the time of the murder. Of the 977 prospective jurors, 29 percent (288) changed their previous conviction decisions to either uncertain or not guilty (see Table 5.2). Thus, it appears that, for the majority of prospective jurors, psychiatric testimony supporting insanity has no effect on their decisions to convict. Indeed, the effect of the total number of changed decisions was non-significant. Among those who changed decisions, however, more than half changed to guilty, a little over one-third changed to uncertain, and about 15 percent changed to not guilty. Changed decisions among jurors who originally indicated uncertainty suggests that, for them, psychiatric testimony has a negative effect and increases the number of decisions to convict.

Table 5.2 Conviction Decisions for All Prospective Jurors When Insanity is Introduced

CONVICTION DECISION WITH INSANITY INTRODUCED		INITIAL CONVICTION DECISION			
		NOT GUILTY	GUILTY	UNCERTAIN	TOTAL
Not Guilty	(N)	3	26	16	45
	(%)	33.3	3.9	5.2	4.6
Guilty		4	540	146	690
		44.4	81.8	47.4	70.6
Uncertain		2	94	146	242
		22.2	14.2	47.4	24.8
Total		9	660	308	977
%		0.9	67.6	31.5	

Wilcoxon test for significance of change = (z = −.387, p = .699).

Two approaches were used in the sentencing portion of this question. First, we examined DPQ original sentencing decisions and compared those to sentences issued after the temporary insanity variable was introduced. Of those who originally imposed the death penalty, 78 (17.4%) changed their minds after hearing psychiatric testimony that the defendant was temporarily insane (see Table 5.3). Conversely, 7 (2.2%) of those who originally provided a sentence other than death subsequently imposed the death penalty where they had not done so before. The end result was a decrease in the number of death sentences to slightly less than a majority after the introduction of psychiatric testimony.

Table 5.3 Sentencing Decisions for DPQ Prospective Jurors When Insanity is Introduced

SENTENCING DECISION WITH INSANITY INTRODUCED		INITIAL SENTENCING DECISION				
		DEATH PENALTY	LIFE	PRISON	OTHER	TOTAL
Death Penalty	(N)	371	4	2	1	378
	(%)	82.6	1.8	2.6	3.6	49.2
Life		68	200	0	1	269
		15.1	88.9	0.0	5.6	35.0
Prison		8	17	71	2	98
		1.8	7.6	93.4	11.1	12.8
Other		2	4	3	14	23
		0.4	1.8	3.9	77.8	3.0
Total		449	225	76	18	768
%		58.5	29.3	9.9	2.3	

Wilcoxon test for significance of change = (z = −7.148, p = .0000).

The second approach to the sentencing issue was to determine whether the prospective jurors would consider a lesser sentence (in a murder case) when the defendant was found to be mentally ill at the time of the offense. Since this particular example did not specify that the event was a *capital* case, it was reasonable to examine the total group of prospective jurors, including DPEs. For the entire group, then, a little over one-third of the respondents considered (but not necessarily imposed) a lesser sentence when the defendant had a mental condition (see Table 5.4). Comparing DPQs to DPEs, it was clear that the DPQs were less likely (31.6%) to consider mental illness a mitigating factor in sentencing than were the DPEs (50.2%).

Table 5.4 Consideration of Lesser Sentence When Mental Illness is Introduced

JUROR GROUP		WOULD CONSIDER LESSER SENTENCE	CHI-SQ*	p
All Jurors	(n = 975)	347 (35.6%)		
DPQ	(n = 768)	243 (31.6%)	4.91	.027
DPE	(n = 207)	104 (50.2%)		

*Chi-square test between DPQ and DPE.

Question 5: *Is there a difference between the conviction decisions of prospective death-qualified and death-excluded jurors once psychiatric information is proffered?*

In answering this question, we created a dichotomy for the conviction variable, resulting in the conviction decision being defined as "guilty" or "not guilty" (the not guilty and uncertain categories were combined). In comparison to the DPQs, the DPEs were less likely to convict, both before and after the introduction of psychiatric information (see Table 5.5). After psychiatric testimony the guilty decisions of the excluded jurors were some 5 percent under their original levels. The same figure for qualified jurors was 5 percent larger than the initial decisions. Considering the original 5 percent differential between the two groups, this resulted in a final 15 percent greater likelihood of conviction by the DPQ group.

Table 5.5 Comparison of DPQ and DPE Conviction Decisions When Insanity is Introduced

JUROR GROUPS		% ORIGINAL CONVICTIONS	% CONVICTIONS POST-INSANITY	p*
DPQ	(n = 768)	68.5	74.0	.163
DPE	(n = 209)	64.1	58.4	.004

*McNemar test for significance of change.
(DPQ = 91 lower ranks, 127 larger ranks, 550 ties)
(DPE = 45 lower ranks, 25 larger ranks, 139 ties)

Under current state statutes, separate jury panels are not used for the guilt and sentencing phases of a capital trial. Therefore, those DPEs who could be included in the guilt phase of a trial will not, of course, be seated. With a conviction dichotomy, then, the dominant effect of psychiatric testimony supporting insanity is to increase the total number of guilty verdicts. In fact, slightly over half of the original not-guilty DPQ jurors (125 of 242) changed their decisions to guilty, resulting in a final three-in-four probability of a guilty verdict.

Question 6: *Does psychiatric information interact with the defendant's characteristics in the conviction or sentencing decisions of prospective death-qualified jurors?*

The same conviction dichotomy was used here as in Question 5 above. The sentencing variable became "death penalty" and "no death penalty" (the life, prison and other categories were combined). Two defendant characteristics were considered: race (or ethnicity) and gender.

Where conviction is concerned, white and black defendants both experienced the same general tendency toward increased guilty verdicts once psychiatric testimony of insanity was introduced (see Table 5.6). For Hispanic defendants, however, there was almost no change in guilty verdicts. There was also a differential effect between males and females, in that guilty verdicts for males increased while those for females remained approximately the same. Thus, male, white, and black defendants seemed to interact with insanity testimony such that the likelihood of conviction was increased.

Table 5.6 Effect of Defendant Characteristics on Conviction and Sentencing

CONVICTION COMPARISON GROUPS	N	A % NOT GUILTY CHANGED TO GUILTY	B ORIGINAL % GUILTY	C % INSANITY INTRODUCED GUILTY	*p CHG B-C
All DPQs	768	51.7	68.5	74.0	.005
White Def.	248	63.3	69.4	78.2	.015
Hispanic Def.	276	42.9	69.6	68.5	.817
Black Def.	237	50.6	66.7	75.9	.006
Female Def.	389	50.9	71.2	73.5	.435
Male Def.	372	52.8	65.9	74.5	.002
SENTENCING COMPARISON GROUPS	N	% DEATH PEN. CHANGED TO NO DP	ORIGINAL % DP	% INSANITY INTRODUCED DP	*p CHG B-C
All DPQs	768	17.4	58.5	49.2	.000
White Def.	247	17.8	52.2	43.7	.000
Hispanic Def.	277	21.9	61.0	48.7	.000
Black Def.	237	12.5	60.8	54.0	.000
Female Def.	390	19.5	53.8	44.4	.000
Male Def.	371	15.9	62.5	53.4	.000

*McNemar test for significance of change.

The critical point in the examination of change in capital sentencing is whether a particular factor influences decisions to sentence to death, not movement among alternative non-death sentences. Thus, an analysis of the effect of race and gender on sentencing after the introduction of insanity testimony focuses on (1) death penalty decisions changed to other sentences and (2) the percentage of original death sentences compared to the final percentage of death sentences.

Where the first point is concerned, the introduction of psychiatric testimony resulted in a decrease in death sentences imposed by the prospective DPQ jurors. Across the three races, Hispanic defendants benefited from the greatest amount of change (21.9%) from death sentences to non-death sentences (see Table 5.6). Conversely, black defendants received the least benefit (12.5%). Females also experienced a greater reduction in death sentences than males (19.5% and 15.9%, respectively).

When the second point was considered and original and post-testimony death sentences were compared, the percentage of death sentences decreased as expected. There were, however, some differentials among the groups. Because white defendants had the lowest percentage of initial death sentences, they constituted the group with the lowest percentage of post-testimony death sentences (43.7%). Minority defendants, especially blacks, had a higher percentage of post-testimony death sentences than did whites. Female defendants benefited by receiving fewer death sentences (44.4%) than did males (53.4%) at the hands of the prospective jurors. In fact, all groups benefited to some degree from psychiatric testimony concerning insanity. Differential death sentence rates among the racial/ethnic groups largely reflected the fact that blacks failed to receive as much benefit from psychiatric testimony as whites and Hispanics. There seemed to be no differential psychiatric testimony effect among males and females since the original and post-testimony differences were approximately the same.

CONCLUSIONS

The findings presented here generally match expectations derived from previous research on insanity and the death penalty. Prospective capital jurors were less willing to trust psychiatrists and psychologists than they were to trust those actors associated with the prosecution. As expected, prospective death-qualified jurors were less trusting of psychiatrists and psychologists than were excludable prospective jurors. Given the propensity of the DPQ group to place greater trust in prosecutorial actors, there is the likelihood that psychiatric testimony on the side of the prosecution would be ascribed more credibility than would psychiatric testimony on the side of the defense. These results, then, seem consonant with the crime control and due process interpretation borrowed from Packer (1967) and advanced by some recent researchers (Fitzgerald & Ellsworth, 1984; Luginbuhl & Crocker, 1983; Thompson et al., 1984). In fact, it appeared that our prospective jurors operated from ideological schema (Luginbuhl & Middendorf, 1988) that went beyond simple *a priori* assessments of the nature of criminal responsibility. The data suggest that, in addition, the schema are inclusive of actors who are perceived to be working for or against the defendant.

Where the effects of insanity testimony are concerned, we considered two areas: conviction and sentencing.[3] When all prospective jurors were considered, we found no significant change in conviction effect as a result of psychiatric testimony on temporary insanity. There was, however, evidence that a substantial number of prospective jurors who had previously been uncertain in their conviction decisions would, upon the introduction of psychiatric testimony, move toward a guilty verdict. While this was somewhat offset by jurors who had initially chosen a guilty verdict and who subsequently moved toward uncertainty, the general effect still served to increase the conviction rate.

Previous research consistently shows that DPQ jurors are conviction-prone.

And, indeed, in our study, there was an increase in DPQ jurors' conviction rate after the introduction of psychiatric testimony. The excludables, on the other hand, decreased their number of convictions, leaving a 15% difference between themselves and the DPQ jurors. These results indicate that psychiatric testimony concerning insanity tends to be detrimental to the interests of a capital defendant and may lead to a small increase in the number of convictions. Further, as opposed to the excludables, the conviction-proneness of prospective DPQ jurors appears to be such that they tend to view temporary insanity as an aggravating, rather than a mitigating, circumstance.

When we asked about the more general effect of mental illness in a non-capital murder case, about a third of the prospective jurors responded that they would consider a lesser sentence. Excludables were much more likely (50.2%) than death-qualified jurors (31.6%) to consider mental illness as a mitigating factor. These results support the findings of Ellsworth et al. (1984) and Luginbuhl and Middendorf (1988).

The possibility of differential effect was examined through the use of a random set of defendant characteristics embedded in a factorial scenario. For this particular analysis, we used the race and gender of the defendant and focused on the death-qualified group. There was evidence of an increased likelihood of conviction for white, black and male defendant groups. However, previous analyses of these data (Williams & McShane, 1987) indicate that the relatively high conviction rate of white defendants is largely due to the presence of young white males, and that other white defendant groups have substantially lower rates. Thus, the results suggest that black defendants are particularly disadvantaged in the conviction phase of a capital trial when psychiatric testimony alleging temporary insanity is used.

Where sentencing is concerned, the result of psychiatric testimony was to produce relatively fewer death sentences for all defendants. Our prospective jurors imposed comparatively lower rates of death sentences for whites and females, both before and after the introduction of psychiatric testimony. While black (and male) death-sentence rates also dropped in post-psychiatric sentencing decisions, black rates dropped proportionately less. This resulted in black defendants having the only death sentence rate over 50 percent. Hispanic defendants achieved the largest reduction in death sentences (12.2%) but, in comparison with whites, their original disadvantaged position left them with a proportionately greater chance of being given the death penalty. Thus, psychiatric testimony alleging insanity appears to have some differential effect which is largely based on a diminished sentencing benefit to black defendants. When this is paired with an increased likelihood of conviction, black defendants emerge as the one group for whom psychiatric testimony has the least benefits.

In sum, the general thrust of these comparisons supports the notion that a crime control/due process schema is, indeed, at play in the minds of prospective jurors. Further, such a schema affects the way psychiatric testimony is perceived and the way in which insanity evidence is received in the conviction and sentencing phases of a capital trial. The introduction of psychiatric testimony at the sentencing phase benefits a defendant, although differentially so, depending upon race/ethnicity and gender. Despite this, the earlier introduction of that testimony at the conviction phase tends to be perceived by prospective death-qualified jurors as adverse information and, thus, is a dangerous ploy for the defense.

NOTES

1   The conviction subquestion read: "Would you vote to convict?" Response categories were "no, not guilty," "no, not guilty because of insanity," "not sure," "yes, guilty," and "not enough information to make a decision." The sentencing subquestion read: "If the person were convicted anyway, would you CHANGE the sentence you gave above? [Note: a criminal jury cannot sentence a person to a mental institution.]" Response categories were "no" and "yes." The question following asked "If yes, what would be the new sentence?" Answers were identical to the sentencing categories provided in the original scenario sentencing question.

2   Possible defendant conditions included: (1) mentally ill at the time of the murder, (2) under severe stress at the time of the murder, (3) forced by someone else into committing the murder, (4) drunk at the time of the murder, (5) on drugs at the time of the murder, (6) on prescribed medicine at the time of the murder, (7) mentally retarded, (8) handicapped, (9) elderly, and (10) 15 years old.

3   We do not claim that these findings are direct evidence of decisions that will be made during actual jury deliberations; we merely present evidence that prospective capital jurors are predisposed to consider psychiatric factors in a certain light. But as others (Ellsworth et al., 1984:82; Luginbuhl & Middendorf, 1988:277-278) have pointed out, research findings strongly suggest that prior beliefs influence decisions made by jurors in actual settings. Certainly, from the psychological literature, one is hard-pressed to deny the effect of preexisting attitudes and mind-sets on behavior. We believe that one would be equally hard-pressed to deny that the attitudes found in this study (and other similar studies) will have no bearing on the way these respondents would behave if called to serve on a capital jury.

REFERENCES

Boehm, V. (1968). "Mr. Prejudice, Miss Sympathy and the Authoritarian Personality: An Application of Psychological Measuring Techniques to the Problem of Jury Bias." *Wisconsin Law Review,* 734-750.

Bronson, E. (1970). "On the Conviction-Proneness and Representativeness of the Death-Qualified Jury: An Empirical Study of Colorado Veniremen." *University of Colorado Law Review,* 42:1-32.

Cook, T. & D.T. Campbell (1979). *Quasi-Experimentation: Design and Analysis Issues for Field Settings*. Skokie, IL: Rand McNally.

Cowen, C., W. Thompson & P. Ellsworth (1984). "The Effects of Death Qualification on Jurors' Predisposition to Convict and on the Quality of Deliberation." *Law and Human Behavior*, 8 (1/2):53-80.

Ellsworth, P., R. Bukaty, C. Cowan & W. Thompson (1984). "The Death-Qualified Jury and the Defense of Insanity." *Law and Human Behavior*, 8 (1/2):81-93.

Fitzgerald, R. & P. Ellsworth (1984). "Due Process vs. Crime Control: Death Qualification and Jury Attitudes." *Law and Human Behavior*, 8 (1/2):31-52.

Goldberg, F. (1970). "Toward Expansion of Witherspoon: Capital Scruples, Jury Bias, and Use of Psychological Data to Raise Presumptions in the Law." *Harvard Civil Rights-Civil Liberties Law Review*, 5:53-69.

Harris, Louis & Associates (1971). *Study No. 2016*. (On file at NAACP Legal Defense Fund, 10 Columbus Circle, New York, NY 10019).

Jurow, G. (1970). "New Data on the Effect of a 'Death-Qualified' Jury in the Guilt Determination Process." *Harvard Law Review*, 84:567-611.

Lerner, M. (1980). *The Belief in a Just World*. New York: Plenum.

Luginbuhl, J. & S. Crocker (1983). "Reluctance of Death Qualified Jurors to Endorse Due Process Guarantees." Paper presented at the annual meeting of the American Psychology-Law Society, Chicago.

Luginbuhl, J. & K. Middendorf (1988). "Death Penalty Beliefs and Jurors' Responses to Aggravating and Mitigating Circumstances in Capital Trials." *Law and Human Behavior*, 12 (3):263-281.

Middendorf, K. & J. Luginbuhl (1981). "Personality and the Death Penalty." Paper presented at the annual meeting of the Southeastern Psychological Association, Atlanta, Georgia.

Moran, G. & J. Comfort (1986). "Neither 'Tentative' Nor 'Fragmentary': Verdict Preference of Impaneled Felony Jurors as a Function of Attitude Toward Capital Punishment." *Journal of Applied Psychology*, 71:146-155.

Rossi, P. & S. Nock (1982). *Measuring Social Judgments*. Beverly Hills: Sage.

Roberts, C., S. Golding & F. Fincham (1987). "Implicit Theories of Criminal Responsibility." *Law and Human Behavior*, 11 (3):207-232.

Rubin, Z. & L. Peplau (1975). "Who Believes in a Just World." *Journal of Social Issues*, 31:65-90.

Simon, R. (1967). *The Jury and the Defense of Insanity*. Boston: Little, Brown.

Thompson, W., C. Cowan, P. Ellsworth & J. Harrington (1984). "Death Penalty Attitudes and Conviction Proneness." *Law and Human Behavior,* 8 (1/2):95-113.

Williams, F. & M. McShane (1987). "Conviction and Sentencing Behavior of Prospective Capital Jurors: A Factorial Scenario Approach." Paper presented at the annual meeting of the American Society of Criminology, Montreal.

CASES

Estelle v. Smith, 451 U.S. 454 (1981).

Hovey v. California, 28 Cal. 3d 1, 616 P.2d 1301, 168 Cal. Rptr. 128 (1980).

Satterwhite v. Texas, 108 S. Ct. 1792 (1988).

Witherspoon v. Illinois, 391 U.S. 510 (1968).

APPENDIX 5-A

WORDING OF FACTORIAL SCENARIO

The description of the defendant in each of the factorial scenarios varied among the 12 combinations of gender (male, female), race (white, black, Hispanic), and age (22, 65). The wording of the scenario was as follows:

You will find a description of a capital crime below. We would like you to read the description and then tell us if, as a juror, you would vote to CONVICT the individual. (This is a fictional crime.)

> A (age) year old, (race) (gender) is charged with capital murder. The crime took place when a masked (gender) entered the unlocked back door of a car with two women in it. At the time the car was stopped at a traffic light. The (gender) pulled out a .38 caliber handgun, put it to the head of the driver and demanded their jewelry and purses. Both of the victims did as they were directed. The (gender) told the driver to pull over next to a deserted lot. The (gender) then shot the driver in the head, killing her instantly. The passenger opened her door and began to run, and was shot once in the shoulder. The offender jumped out of the car and ran away with about $700 worth of money and jewelry. The passenger was taken to the hospital and recovered after surgery. Two days after the crime, the police arrested the defendant in the parking lot of a pawn shop after a suspicious clerk recognized the items from a robbery report. A search of the defendant's apartment turned up a ski mask and a pistol which matched the one used in the crime. In addition, the defendant's height and weight was generally the same as that described by the surviving victim.

As a member of the jury, would you vote to convict this person?

☐ No   ☐ Not sure   ☐ Yes   ☐ Not enough information to make a decision

If this person (no prior record) were convicted by the jury, what type of sentence would you recommend and for how long? (PLEASE CHOOSE ONLY ONE SENTENCE TYPE BELOW.)

☐ Death penalty
☐ Life in prison
☐ A prison sentence of ___ years
☐ A jail sentence of ___ years (maximum of 24 months)
☐ A probation sentence of ___ years (maximum of 10 years)

6

Return of the Dead:
An Update on the Status of *Furman-*
Commuted Death Row Inmates*

Gennaro F. Vito
School of Justice Administration
University of Louisville

Pat Koester
National Clearinghouse on Jails and Prisons

Deborah G. Wilson
School of Justice Administration
University of Louisville

INTRODUCTION

On March 1, 1989, the NAACP Legal Defense Fund reported that the death row inmate population in the United States stood at 2,186 and 106 inmates have been executed since the reinstitution of capital punishment in 1977 (*Death Row, U.S.A.*, 1989). Clearly, the rate of executions is not keeping up with the influx of new death row inmates. The implication has always been that these inmates are either too dangerous to be handled in another fashion or that their crimes deserve the ultimate penalty. In *Furman v. Georgia* (408 U.S. 238, 1972), the U.S. Supreme Court declared the capital punishment system then in operation unconstitutional and thus commuted the death sentences of over 600 inmates (Greenberg, 1982). This decision gave criminologists the opportunity to examine whether murderers must be executed to protect the public.

* This paper was developed under a research completion grant from the University of Louisville under the sponsorship of Dr. Donald C. Swain. Points of view and opinions expressed in this paper are those of the authors and do not necessarily represent the official position of the University of Louisville.

89

In 1988, we published our initial findings on the status of *Furman*-commuted inmates who were paroled from Kentucky institutions (Vito & Wilson, 1988). At that time, we noted that we planned to conduct an analysis of this group on a nationwide basis. As a result of the efforts of the National Clearinghouse on Jails and Prisons, this analysis is now complete and it is possible to make some overall assessment of the parole performance of this group of inmates who came back from the dead.

LITERATURE REVIEW

There have been very few studies of convicted murderers who either have had their death sentences commuted or were released on parole after serving a portion of a life sentence. Yet, there are some pertinent points of comparison to be made between the few earlier studies and our present undertaking. Giardini and Farrow (1952) present findings concerning both paroled and commuted capital offenders from 22 states over a period of approximately 38 years (N = 197). They found that 129 offenders were still on parole, 34 had cleared supervision, 11 died, 5 absconded, 7 committed technical violations, and 11 committed new offenses but no new murders. The total reincarceration rate was 9.7 percent.

Stanton (1969) conducted a study of the characteristics and recidivism rates of 63 New York State parolees released between July, 1930 and December 31, 1961. Through 1962, only one member of this group of paroled first degree murderers had been returned to prison for a new felony conviction (burglary). In addition, two offenders were returned on a technical violation for a total reincarceration rate of 9.8 percent (Stanton, 1969:153).

In more recent research endeavors, Donnelly and Bala (1984) did a five-year follow-up on 66 murderers paroled from New York prisons in 1977 and determined that 22.6 percent of the offenders had been reincarcerated. Similarly, Wallerstedt (1984) reported that the median reincarceration rate for paroled homicide offenders from five states (Michigan, 1978; Nebraska, 1980; New York, 1976; Oregon, 1978; & Rhode Island, 1979) was approximately 27.3 percent.

However, these studies did not focus on offenders who had actually faced a death sentence. Prior to the Kentucky *Furman* research, three analyses considered the performance of death row inmates who had their sentences commuted. In Great Britain, Coker and Martin (1985) tracked murderers who were under a death sentence and were paroled following commutation. They discovered that 65 of the 239 offenders committed a new crime, 15 of which were violent offenses including two murders. One of the murders was committed after a parolee had been committed to a mental hospital. All of the offenders who committed new crimes were returned to prison for a total reincarceration rate of 27.2 percent.

Similarly, Marquart and Sorensen (1988) have presented a detailed analysis of the 47 members of the Texas *Furman* population. In addition to the figures presented later in this chapter, the authors also conducted an analysis of the prison behavior of these inmates following their release from death row confinement—a significant contribution to the literature on this subject. Although prison officials felt that these inmates presented a clear and present threat to the security of the institution, the research determined that the group committed a few minor rule violations and did not kill any other inmates or staff.

Finally, in September of 1988, ABC News presented a special report entitled "Life After Death Row." This documentary followed the parole performance of 40 (out of 103 or 38.8%) California death row inmates whose sentences were commuted to life when, just prior to the *Furman* decision, the state supreme court declared the death penalty statute unconstitutional. Included among this group were such infamous murderers as Charles Manson and Sirhan Sirhan (not paroled) and the "Onion Field" killers (who were paroled). In terms of recidivism, ABC reporter Tom Jariel stated that four of the 40 parolees had been returned to prison (10%) and one of the recidivists (Robert Lee Massie) committed another homicide on parole.[1]

In sum, previous research on both murderers sentenced to life in prison and former death row inmates reveals that their parole performance runs counter to the conventional view that such offenders are exceptionally dangerous. Rates of reincarceration were below the "30 percent threshold" found in many studies of probation and parole (Allen, Eskridge, Latessa & Vito, 1985:260). The rate of repeat murder was decidedly low—two in the British study and one in the California and Texas groups. In addition, the Texas analysis indicates that the *Furman* group did not cause trouble in the institution when they returned to the general population. Overall, the results of these studies indicate that murderers do not appear to represent a great risk in prison or in the community following their release on parole.

METHODOLOGY

The data presented here are from a survey conducted by the National Clearinghouse on Prisons and Jails. This survey was underway at the time we were working on the Kentucky analysis. Simultaneously, Marquart and Sorensen (1988) were pursuing their study of the Texas *Furman* group. Eventually, these various parties became aware of each other and shared their research information.[2]

The survey was conducted in 1987. All of the states with *Furman* inmates were sent copies of the questionnaire/letter via the corrections department. The Clearinghouse survey consisted of eight questions:

1. At the time these sentences were commuted from death to life imprisonment, what standards were set for determining when these prisoners would be eligible for parole?

2. How many of these prisoners have been paroled?

3. How many of those paroled have regained their full civil and political rights?

4. How many of those paroled have committed further offenses? Please break down any offenses by type of offense.

5. How many of those paroled have been returned to prison? On what types of sentences?

6. How many have not been paroled?

7. How many of those not paroled have committed violent offenses in prison?

8. Have any of the inmates died, been killed, or committed suicide either in or out of prison?

Questionnaires were returned to the Atlanta office of the National Clearinghouse on Jails and Prisons and copies of the responses were provided to the University of Louisville for data analysis.

RESEARCH FINDINGS

The overall parole and recidivism rates from the 26 states responding to the survey are presented in Table 6.1. Of the total number of living *Furman*-commuted inmates at the time of the survey (N = 457), 185 (40.6%) were granted parole. Excluding the parolees who died while on supervision (N = 8), the reincarceration rate was 19.7 percent.

As indicated in Table 6.1, the parole rates of the *Furman* inmates ranged from a high of 100 percent (Colorado, New Hampshire) to a low of zero (Maryland, New York, Connecticut, Kansas, and Nebraska). However, these rates must be interpreted with caution. It is impossible to determine from these figures whether a state was particularly "lenient" or "harsh" in its parole stance toward these inmates. There are at least two reasons why such conclusions would be premature. First, since these inmates were considered at various points in time, it is unlikely that any one particular state parole board was responsible for making decisions for the entire group. Second, we cannot directly compare one state to another because we do not have the necessary background data on each and every case. For example, if such a study was undertaken, we could find that the states paroled those *Furman* inmates who were the "best risks" in terms of prior record, employment history, and other factors which have been demonstrated as relevant to the probability of success on parole. This is not a study of parole board decision-making,[3] and without such information, a state-by-state comparison would be methodologically imprecise and theoretically immature.

Table 6.1 Status of *Furman*-Commuted Death Row Inmates, 1987

State[a]	Cases	Paroled[b]	Recidivists[c]
Florida	96	36 (38.7%)	8 (22.9%)
Ohio	49	20 (43.5%)	5 (26.3%)
Texas	47	31 (70.4%)	6 (20.7%)
Georgia	42	23 (56.1%)	2 (8.7%)
Alabama	27	9 (37.5%)	1 (11.1%)
Pennsylvania	25	4 (16.0%)	0
Maryland	23	0	0
Kentucky	22	19 (90.5%)	6 (31.6%)
Massachusetts	21	2 (11.1%)	0
Tennessee	16	6 (37.5%)	0
Missouri	16	7 (46.7%)	3 (42.9%)
Oklahoma	15	1 (6.7%)	0
North Carolina	11	2 (18.2%)	0
South Carolina	11	8 (88.9%)	1 (14.3%)
Indiana	9	1 (11.1%)	N/A
Washington	9	3 (33.3%)	0
Nevada	8	1 (14.3%)	0
Arkansas	6	3 (50.0%)	0
New York	5	0	N/A
Utah	5	3 (60.0%)	1 (33.3%)
Connecticut	4	0	0
Delaware	3	2 (66.6%)	0
Colorado	2	2 (100%)	1 (50.0%)
Kansas	2	0	N/A
New Hampshire	2	2 (100%)	1 (50.0%)
Nebraska	2	0	N/A
TOTALS	478	185 (40.0%)	35 (19.7%)
ADJUSTED TOTALS	457	177	

[a]The following states did not respond to the survey (N of *Furman* cases): Illinois (31); Louisiana (36); Mississippi (9); and Virginia (12).

[b]The rates of parole are adjusted for the number of inmates who died in prison (N = 21): Alabama, Florida, Massachusetts, Ohio and Texas (3 each); South Carolina (2); and Georgia, Kentucky, Missouri and Nevada (1 each).

[c]The recidivism rates are adjusted to account for the number of parolees who died following their release but did not die during the commission of a new offense (N = 8): Texas (2) and Arkansas, Florida, Indiana, Pennsylvania, South Carolina, and Ohio (1 each).

This survey also considered, as did Marquart and Sorensen (1988), the institutional behavior of the 272 *Furman*-commuted inmates who were not paroled (excluding Texas). The survey uncovered a total of 25 violent offenses (11% of the total number of institutional violations) committed by this group following their return to the general prison population. The offenses varied but typically included escape, assault, and robbery. For example, in Florida, six inmates were convicted of escape and one was sentenced for murder (of an inmate). In Georgia, two assaults and two escapes were committed by *Furman* inmates.

The most startling incidents of institutional violence took place in Ohio. One *Furman* inmate (who was never paroled) killed a correctional officer during a hostage incident in 1973 and was sentenced to life in prison. A second Ohio inmate was released in 1981 and returned on a parole violation (weapon possession) in 1982. He subsequently murdered a prison shop supervisor at Lucasville, was sentenced to death a second time, and is presently on death row awaiting execution. These findings, coupled with the murder of the Florida inmate, clearly indicate that the level of institutional violence reported for the *Furman* cohort is much more serious than the violations reported by Marquart and Sorensen (1988) among the Texas inmates.

Table 6.2 Number of Recidivists[a] by Type of Offense

Type of Offense	Number	Percent
Parole Violation	12	34.3
Burglary	6	17.1
Drug Offenses	5	14.2
Other Property	4	11.4
Murder	3	8.6
Robbery	3	8.6
Rape	1	2.9
Kidnapping	1	2.9
TOTAL	35	100

[a]The operational definition of recidivism is *returned to prison (reincarcerated)*.

Regarding the parole performance of the *Furman*-commuted group (N = 177, excluding those who died while on supervision), 29 parolees (16.4%) cleared supervision and regained (in applicable states) their civil rights.[4] As Table 6.2 shows, the majority of recidivists (total N = 35) were returned to prison for a violation of their conditions of parole (34.3%). Another nine parolees (25.6%) were reincarcerated for property or drug offenses. Nonviolent offenses (parole violations, burglary, drug offenses, and other property crimes) accounted for 77 percent of the total recidivism rate.[5]

However, some *Furman*-commuted recidivists (8/177 = 4.5%) did commit violent crimes. This subgroup was responsible for three murders, three robberies, one rape, and a kidnapping. Marquart and Sorensen (1988) report that one of the murders was committed by a Texas inmate during an out of state, family argument after which the parolee committed suicide. We chose to count this homicide as a recidivist offense but not to include the prison homicides from Ohio and Florida since the murderers were not on parole.

These offenses and their impact upon the citizenry cannot be discounted, but the level of seriousness is comparable to that revealed in other studies. For example, in the British study by Coker and Martin, recidivists (65/239 = 27.2%) were responsible for 15 violent offenses including two murders (repeat homicide rate = 0.8%). The repeat homicide rate for the *Furman* parolees was 1.6 percent (3/185). This repeat homicide rate appears to be lower than that generated by current death row inmates. A recent report on the prior record of the death row inmates by the Bureau of Justice Statistics (1988:8) reveals that 11.2 percent of the group (10% of the whites and 12.8% of the blacks) had a "prior homicide conviction" history and had therefore committed murder a second time. This rate was much lower in Vito and Keil's (1988) analysis of 864 convicted Kentucky homicide offenders (between 1976 and 1986). They reported that only 2.6 percent of the Kentucky offenders (N = 22) had a prior conviction for a capital offense.

Does this mean that the current death row offender is more deadly and dangerous than his/her earlier counterparts? Perhaps, but it is difficult to speculate why this would be true. It may be that the current offender is more likely to be involved with drug abuse or that the death row experience of the *Furman*-commuted inmates had a deterrent effect upon their parole behavior.

The reincarceration rates reported from the various studies are presented in Table 6.3. The rate of the *Furman* group falls in the middle of the range of reported reincarceration rates of paroled murderers.

Table 6.3 Comparison of Reincarceration Rates: *Furman* Cohort Versus Other Studies of Paroled Murderers

Study	Reincarceration Rate
Giardini & Farrow (1952)	9.7%
Stanton (1969)	9.7%
Donnally & Bala (1984)	27.3%
Wallerstedt (1984)	22.6%
Coker & Martin (1985)	27.2%
ABC News Report (1988)	10.0%
Marquart & Sorensen (1988)	25.0%
Vito & Wilson (1988)	29.0%
Furman Cohort (1988)	19.7%

CONCLUSION

The *Furman* parolees have performed better than expected, though in the absence of detailed information on each inmate, this conclusion must remain tentative. Certain characteristics (e.g., employment, sobriety, family support) may separate the parole successes from the failures. This is certainly an issue for future research. Whether the murder of three citizens, one inmate, and two correctional officials constitutes an acceptable level of risk is difficult to answer. Given the experience of this cohort, however, it is clear that societal protection from convicted capital murderers is not greatly enhanced by the death penalty.

The results of this research are not likely to be accepted without skepticism. In this regard, we offer as a postscript the most recent experience of Kentucky, the state which served as the cornerstone for our research effort.

Recently, two more *Furman* inmates were released on parole.[6] These brothers, William and Narvel Tinsley, were convicted and sentenced to die for the murders of two Louisville police officers. At their first parole board hearing, members of the victim's families and the Louisville police department appeared and made their feelings known. At that time, both Tinsley brothers were denied parole because of the "seriousness of the crime and the severity of prior record" (*Louisville Courier-Journal*, 1987).

By September of 1988, William Tinsley had been released and Narvel Tinsley was awaiting release from a forestry camp. Board members stated that the key elements in their decision were that "without question...these were not the same men who had come into the institution;" that both brothers had developed vocational and academic skills and would be working and living near family after release (O'Doherty, 1988a).

The public outcry was not long in coming. In Louisville, a crowd of 300 people, including several Louisville police officers and a state court of appeals judge who originally presided over the Tinsleys' case in 1971, protested the parole board's decision (O'Doherty, 1988b). They were particularly incensed that the decision was made without input from the victims' families. State law requires that the parole board notify victims or family members of only the first hearing. When the chairman of the board was asked for the reason for release, he repeated that the board had decided that the Tinsley's "had become good parole risks" through education and good work records, and they expressed an understanding of the crime and remorse for it.[7] Later, the parole board chairman argued that the board "gave more notice than legally required" before granting parole to the Tinsleys and that board members "knew full well not everyone would agree with our decision" (*Louisville Courier-Journal*, 1989).

The point is that the Tinsleys do fit the profile of the Kentucky *Furman* inmate who succeeded on parole (see Vito & Wilson, 1988:106-108). Nevertheless, they were paroled despite great protest. Whether the emotionality of paroling convicted capital murderers can be overcome on a national basis is a question that still awaits an answer.

NOTES

[1] In previous published accounts, Robert Lee Massie was erroneously listed as a member of the *Furman* cohort (see Urofsky, 1984:569-570; Vito & Wilson, 1988:109). If the California Supreme Court had not overturned these death sentences, the California inmates would be the largest segment of the *Furman* cohort.

[2] Marquart and Sorensen also are continuing their research on the entire *Furman* cohort.

[3] For two excellent examples of the levels of complexity involved in studying parole board decision-making, see Bonham, Janeksela, and Bardo (1986); and Pogrebin, Poole, and Regoli (1986).

[4] Unfortunately, we do not have data on the length of the follow-up period for the entire cohort, but perhaps the figure from the Kentucky subgroup (mean = 42 months) can be considered typical. Long-term studies of recidivism rates (Kitchener, Schmidt & Glaser, 1977; Hoffman & Stone-Meierhoffer, 1980) have consistently demonstrated that the length of the follow-up period is a significant factor in the size of the percentage. In general, the rates will increase with time but it must be kept in mind that a technical violation (often the most common reason for a return to prison) is impossible after the parolee has cleared supervision (usually five years after release).

[5] We assume that the remaining 113 *Furman* parolees were still under supervision at the end of the research period.

[6] There are two more *Furman* inmates in Kentucky. One is not eligible for release since he also was sentenced to life without parole (in addition to death) for rape under the Kentucky code in force at that time (KRS 435.090) (see Vito & Wilson, 1988:103). The second inmate received a stay of execution in 1963 and has been before the parole board several times since his sentence was commuted to life in prison in 1974. At his last hearing, he was given a five-year deferment. Therefore, he will not be eligible for release until 1992.

[7] Between the first and second appearance of the Tinsleys, the chairmanship of the parole board changed and the former chair was removed from the board.

REFERENCES

Allen, H.E., C.W. Eskridge, E.J. Latessa & G.F. Vito (1985). *Probation and Parole in America*. New York, NY: The Free Press.

Bonham, G., G. Janeksela & J. Bardo (1986). "Predicting the Parole Decision in Kansas via Discriminant Analysis." *Journal of Criminal Justice*, 14:123-134.

Bureau of Justice Statistics Bulletin (1988). "Capital Punishment 1987." Washington, DC: U.S. Department of Justice (July).

Coker, J.B. & J.P. Martin (1985). *Licensed to Live*. Oxford: Basil Blackwell.

Conrad, J.P. (1985). "News of the Future." *Federal Probation,* 49(December):60-62.

Death Row, U.S.A. (1989). New York: NAACP Legal Defense and Education Fund, Inc. (March 1).

Donnelly, H.C. & G. Bala (1984). *1977 Releases: Five-Year Post-Release Follow-up.* Albany, NY: Department of Correctional Services.

Giardini, G.I. & R.G. Farrow (1952). "The Paroling of Capital Offenders. *The Annals,* 284:85-94.

Greenberg, J. (1982). "Capital Punishment as a System." *The Yale Law Journal,* 91:908-936.

Hoffman, P.B. & B. Stone-Meierhoffer (1980). "Reporting Recidivism Rates: The Criterion and Follow-up Issues." *Journal of Criminal Justice,* 8(1):53-60.

Kitchener, H., A.K. Schmidt & D. Glaser (1977). "How Persistent is Post-Prison Success?" *Federal Probation,* 41(January):9-14.

Louisville Courier-Journal (1987). "Brothers Who Killed Two Police Officers Are Denied Parole." March 21, p. a13.

————— (1989). "Police Groups Urge Wider Notification of Parole Hearings." February 22, p. b3.

Marquart, J.W. & J.R. Sorensen (1988). "Institutional and Post-Release Behavior of the Texas *Furman*-Commuted Inmates." *Criminology,* 26(4):677-693.

O'Doherty, M. (1988a). "Brothers Who Killed Police Deserved Parole, Board Says." *Louisville Courier-Journal,* September 28, pp. a1, a12.

————— (1988b). "Police, Judge Protest Parole For Two Killers Once Sentenced to Die." *Louisville Courier-Journal,* October 1, pp. a7, a10.

Pogrebin, M.R., E.D. Poole & R. Regoli (1986). "Parole Decision-Making in Colorado." *Journal of Criminal Justice,* 14(2):147-156.

Stanton, J.M. (1969). "Murderers on Parole." *Crime and Delinquency,* 15:149-155.

Urofsky, M.I. (1984). "A Right To Die: Termination of Appeal for Condemned Prisoners." *Journal of Criminal Law and Criminology,* 75:553-582.

Vito, G.F. & T.J. Keil (1988). "Capital Sentencing in Kentucky: An Analysis of Post-*Gregg* Outcomes." *Journal of Criminal Law and Criminology,* 79:301-321.

Vito, G.F. & D.G. Wilson (1988). "Back from the Dead: Tracking the Progress of Kentucky's *Furman*-Commuted Death Row Population." *Justice Quarterly,* 5:101-111.

Wallerstedt, J.F. (1984). *Bureau of Justice Statistics Special Report: Returning to Prison.* Washington, DC: U.S. Department of Justice.

7

Comparison of the Dead: Attributes and Outcomes of *Furman*-Commuted Death Row Inmates in Kentucky and Ohio*

Gennaro F. Vito
School of Justice Administration
University of Louisville

Deborah G. Wilson
School of Justice Administration
University of Louisville

Edward J. Latessa
Department of Criminal Justice
University of Cincinnati

INTRODUCTION

Until recently, the literature on the death penalty debate has overlooked the experience of death row inmates whose sentences were commuted by *Furman v. Georgia* (408 U.S. 238, 1972). In addition to the previous chapter in this volume, a preliminary analysis of the entire *Furman*-commuted group, the *Furman* cohorts in Texas and Kentucky have been examined. Our research on this topic continues with a comparison of the experience of two states, Kentucky and Ohio. The

* The authors express their appreciation to John Wigginton, Secretary of the Kentucky Corrections Cabinet; Richard Seiter, former Director of the Ohio Department of Rehabilitation and Correction; George Wilson, former Secretary of the Kentucky Corrections Cabinet and present Director of the Ohio Department of Rehabilitation and Correction; and to Stephan W. Van Dine, Chief, and Evalyn C. Parks, of the Bureau of Planning and Research of the Ohio Department of Rehabilitation and Correction.

This paper was developed under a research completion grant from the University of Louisville under the sponsorship of President Donald C. Swain. The opinions and conclusions expressed in this paper are exclusively those of the authors and do not represent the official positions of the Kentucky Corrections Cabinet, the Ohio Department of Rehabilitation and Correction, or the University of Louisville.

purpose of this chapter is to compare the case and offender characteristics, attributes of victims, system practices, and parole performance of the *Furman* inmates from these contiguous states. A review of the similarities and differences between these two cohorts will allow us to better understand the factors that account for the parole performance of these inmates.

The Kentucky and Texas studies demonstrated that the *Furman*-commuted inmates have not posed a dramatic threat. In Texas, Marquart and Sorensen (1988) reported that the *Furman* inmates committed few institutional violations and did not kill other inmates or staff following commutation. On parole, 19 percent of the 37 *Furman* parolees were reincarcerated and one parolee (2.7%) committed murder and suicide.

The Kentucky research yielded similar parole performance results. Twenty-nine percent of the 17 *Furman* parolees were reincarcerated. Eighteen percent of the group was reincarcerated for a new offense. The most serious new offense was armed robbery. No inmates, staff, or citizens were killed by the Kentucky *Furman* cohort.

METHODOLOGY

The NAACP Legal Defense Fund provided the list of cases for each state (also see Marquart & Sorensen, 1988:681). The list indicated that the number of *Furman* inmates in Kentucky was 21 and in Ohio, 63. However, our review of the records produced different totals. From our review we discovered that, in Ohio, the number of *Furman* inmates was 49 and in Kentucky, 23. The discrepancy in the totals for Kentucky has been discussed elsewhere (Vito & Wilson, 1988:103); the Ohio results require some clarification. We were unable to locate six of the Ohio files. Two of the files were of inmates who had been paroled after they were transferred to an institution out of state. Another file was of an inmate who was classified as a "hideaway," meaning that his file was inaccessible for security reasons. We simply were unable to locate the other three inmate files. In addition, we discovered that the death sentences of four inmates were commuted for reasons other than the *Furman* decision, two inmates died in prison, one had been executed in 1958, and one inmate had escaped from an institution for the criminally insane. For these reasons, our Ohio analysis focuses upon the records and experiences of 49 *Furman* inmates. The total number of Kentucky and Ohio inmates examined in this study is 72, which represents approximately 14 percent of the total population of persons sentenced to die for murder at the time of the *Furman* decision.

All information concerning the *Furman* inmates from Kentucky and Ohio was obtained from case records maintained by the Kentucky Corrections Cabinet and the Ohio Department of Rehabilitation and Correction. Data on the offense and the offender were collected from the presentence investigation reports contained in these files. In addition, newspaper accounts and other official reports on the offense helped to clarify the nature and extent of the crime. Parole decision results as well as performance data also were acquired from case files.

The offense variables considered in this study are those which must be present under current Kentucky law in order for the prosecution to seek the death penalty (aggravating circumstances) or those which may provide an exculpatory explanation for the homicide (mitigating circumstances). In addition to the legal criteria, other variables (e.g., "Was the murder committed to silence the victim?") reflect the relative heinousness of the offense. Thus, the use of this framework provides a mechanism to compare both the heinousness and legal seriousness of the homicides committed by these offenders.

RESEARCH FINDINGS

In the following analysis, five different comparisons are made. The first involves the circumstances surrounding the offense itself; the second, the characteristics of the offenders; the third, the attributes of the victims; the fourth, system practices; and the fifth, parole performance. Regarding original offense characteristics, Table 7.1 shows the many similarities between the two cohorts. The only statistically significant difference between the states is that a higher percentage of the Ohio inmates (44.7%) than their Kentucky counterparts (8.7%) used multiple shots to dispatch their victims. The concurrent offense variable reveals that the majority of both the Kentucky and Ohio homicides were committed during the course of an armed robbery. Though in the remaining categories case numbers are too small to produce meaningful differences, the Ohio inmates were just slightly more likely to be charged with a concurrent sex offense or burglary. The measures of heinousness reveal that the Kentucky offenders were more likely to torture their victim, while the Ohio cases featured mutilation of the body. The groups were approximately equal in the likelihood that they would commit "execution-style" murders or kill persons without any apparent provocation.

Table 7.2 shows that the demographic and criminal history variables of the two cohorts are comparable. They were roughly the same age at the time of the homicide with about nine years of education. On average, members of both cohorts had about one prior felony arrest, conviction, and incarceration. Both cohorts had one member with a prior murder conviction.

Table 7.1 Offense Characteristics: Kentucky and Ohio Death Row Inmates Whose Sentences Were Commuted by *Furman v. Georgia*

Variable	Kentucky	Ohio
USED MULTIPLE SHOTS	2 (8.7%)	21 (44.7%)*
MURDER COMMITED IN CONJUNCTION WITH:		
ROBBERY	13 (56.5%)	28 (58.3%)
RAPE	1 (4.3%)	4 (8.3%)
SODOMY	0 (0.0%)	2 (4.2%)
BURGLARY	1 (4.3%)	3 (6.3%)
EXECUTION-STYLE MURDER	7 (30.4%)	14 (29.8%)
MURDER COMMITTED WITHOUT APPARENT PROVOCATION	17 (73.9%)	36 (76.6%)
MURDER FEATURES TORTURE OF VICTIM	2 (9.1%)	1 (2.1%)
BODY MUTILATED	0 (0.0%)	4 (8.5%)

*Chi-square value is statistically significant at the .05 level or less.

Table 7.2 Offender Characteristics: Kentucky and Ohio Death Row Inmates Whose Sentences Were Commuted by *Furman v. Georgia*

Variable	Mean	t-value	p-value
AGE OF OFFENDER (AT OFFENSE)[a]			
Kentucky	24.41		
Ohio	27.56	1.45	.152
HIGHEST GRADE COMPLETED			
Kentucky	9.83		
Ohio	9.19	0.95	.344
NUMBER OF PRIOR FELONY ARRESTS			
Kentucky	1.87		
Ohio	1.93	0.15	.881
NUMBER OF PRIOR FELONY CONVICTIONS			
Kentucky	0.87		
Ohio	1.41	1.48	.142
NUMBER OF PREVIOUS FELONY INCARCERATIONS			
Kentucky	1.09		
Ohio	1.02	0.17	.867

[a]None of the inmates were juveniles at the time of the offense.

However, as shown in Table 7.3, the general pattern of prior criminal offenses was somewhat different in the two cohorts. The Kentucky group had a significantly higher percentage of inmates with a prior history of violent offenses. The Ohio group was more likely to have no prior criminal record, but it also had almost five times as many persons under probation or parole supervision at the time of the murder. Finally, concerning mitigating circumstances, a greater percentage of the Ohio offenders had mental problems or were intoxicated when the murder was committed.

Table 7.3 Aggravating and Mitigating Circumstances in the Cases of Kentucky and Ohio Death Row Inmates Whose Sentences Were Commuted by *Furman v. Georgia*

Variable	Kentucky	Ohio
	N %	N %
NO PRIOR CRIMINAL RECORD	1 (4.2%)	13 (27.7%)
HISTORY OF VIOLENT OFFENSES[a]	15 (65.2%)	8 (17.8%)*
OFFENDER UNDER SUPERVISION AT THE TIME OF THE OFFENSE		
Probation	1 (4.3%)	4 (12.9%)
Parole	2 (8.6%)	14 (45.2%)
None	20 (87.1%)	31 (41.9%)
EVIDENCE OF MENTAL DISEASE	0 (0.0%)	7 (15.2%)
EVIDENCE OF INTOXICATION	4 (18.2%)	15 (33.3%)

[a]The Kentucky and Ohio cohorts each had one offender with a prior murder conviction.
*Chi-square value significant at the .05 level or less.

Table 7.4 contains data on the attributes of the victims of the two cohorts. The mean number of victims per case and the percentage of cases with multiple victims are nearly identical. The Ohio victims were slightly older than those in Kentucky. The Kentucky homicides produced more police officer victims (41% of the cases) than the Ohio homicides (8.3% of the cases plus the murder of one correctional officer).

In several ways, the Ohio offenders committed homicides which might be considered more abhorrent than those in Kentucky. The Ohio cohort was significantly more likely to murder females. In addition, the Ohio inmates more often used multiple shots to kill their victims, were more likely to commit the offense in the victim's home, and were more likely to kill to "silence" the victim to prevent testimony against the offender.

Table 7.4 Attributes of the Victims of the Death Row Inmates Whose Sentences Were Commuted by *Furman v. Georgia*

I. Variable	Mean	t-value	Probability
NUMBER OF MURDER VICTIMS			
Kentucky (N = 30)	1.30		
Ohio (N = 63)	1.34	0.20	.844
AGE OF VICTIM			
Kentucky	32.06		
Ohio	41.21	1.61	.116

II. Variable	Kentucky Inmates	Ohio Inmates	Chi-square
MULTIPLE VICTIMS			
Yes	4 (17.4%)	7 (14.6%)	__a
No	19 (82.6%)	41 (85.4%)	
POLICE VICTIM[b]			
Yes	9 (40.9%)	4 (8.3%)	__a
No	13 (59.1%)	44 (91.7%)	
VICTIM KILLED AT HOME			
Yes	1 (4.3%)	16 (33.3%)	
No	22 (95.7%)	32 (66.7%)	5.67[c]
MURDER INTENDED TO SILENCE THE VICTIM			
Yes	3 (13.0%)	21 (44.7%)	
No	20 (87.0%)	26 (55.3%)	5.52[c]
SEX OF VICTIM			
Male	19 (82.6%)	25 (51.0%)	
Female	4 (17.4%)	24 (49.0%)	5.31[c]
VICTIM-OFFENDER RELATIONSHIP			
Known	5 (21.7%)	19 (40.4%)	
Stranger	18 (78.3%)	28 (59.6%)	1.64
RACE OF VICTIM			
White	20 (95.2%)	17 (89.5%)	__a
Black	1 (4.8%)	2 (10.5%)	

[a]Chi-square could not be computed for this variable.
[b]One of the Ohio victims was a correctional officer.
[c]Chi-square value significant at the .05 level or less.

The remaining two variables did not involve statistically significant differences, but the Kentucky cohort killed a higher percentage of "stranger" (persons completely unknown to the offender) victims.

The issue of racial discrimination has always been a central question in the administration of the death penalty. For this reason, we examined the interaction between the race of the victim and the race of the offender in each state. As Table 7.5 reveals, neither death row cohort killed a significant number of blacks. The killers of whites were predominant. White offenders who killed blacks did not find their way to death row in either state. In an indirect fashion, this finding constitutes evidence of discrimination by the race of the victim. In fact, such racial discrimination was one of the central issues in the *Furman* decision. Research conducted in each state has demonstrated that this pattern has clearly persisted. Studies of both Kentucky (Vito & Keil, 1988) and Ohio (Bowers & Pierce, 1980) have demonstrated that blacks who kill whites were significantly more likely to receive a death sentence in the post-*Gregg* era. Therefore, the pattern of racial discrimination in death sentencing in both states appears to be unremitting.

Table 7.5 Racial Interactions Between the Victims and the Kentucky and Ohio Death Row Inmates Whose Sentences Were Commuted by *Furman v. Georgia*

Race of the Offender	Race of the Victim	
Kentucky	**White**	**Black**
White	13 (100%)	0 (0.0%)
Black	7 (87.5%)	1 (12.0%)
Ohio		
White	12(100%)	0 (0.0%)
Black	5 (71.4%)	2 (28.6%)

The differences in the operation of the two capital punishment systems seem to indicate that the Ohio capital punishment system was more harsh than that of Kentucky. In Kentucky, governors routinely granted inmates a stay of execution during this period. The last inmate electrocution was on March 2, 1962. In fact, a legislative committee under the direction of Governor Ned Breathitt recommended the abolition of capital punishment in Kentucky (Vito & Keil, 1988:492).

Table 7.6 provides data on some of the system practices for each cohort. The statistically significant differences are that the Ohio cohort had a greater number of stays of execution and spent about twice as long in prison before release on parole than the Kentucky cohort. The Ohio inmates had an average of 1.25 stays of execution before their death sentences were commuted. The number of stays ranged from one to four, and 33 of the 49 Ohio inmates (67.3%) had at least one stay of execution. If the *Furman* decision had not overturned the Ohio death sentences, most of these inmates would have been executed. Only one of the Kentucky *Furman* inmates had a stay of execution. To date, this inmate has not been paroled. While Kentucky inmates spent more time, on the average, on death row (approximately 13 months) than their Ohio counterparts, the Ohio parolees served an average of four years longer in prison until release (11.3 versus 7.3) than the Kentucky cohorts. The overall conclusion is that the Ohio inmates were closer to death by execution.

Table 7.6 System Characteristics: Capital Punishment in Kentucky and Ohio Prior to *Furman v. Georgia*

Variable	Mean	t-value	p-value
NUMBER OF STAYS OF EXECUTION			
Kentucky	0.87		
Ohio	1.25	4.97	.000*
DAYS ON DEATH ROW (UNTIL COMMUTATION)			
Kentucky	1699.48		
Ohio	1248.54	1.56	.124
DAYS UNTIL PAROLE			
Kentucky	2653.63		
Ohio	4106.65	3.48	.001*

*t-value significant at the .05 level or less.

The parole performance of the two cohorts is illustrated in Table 7.7. The rate of parole was twice as great for the Kentucky cohort. In Kentucky, only one of the *Furman* inmates who was eligible was not paroled.[1] In Ohio, 20 of the 49 inmates (40.8%) were paroled. As indicated in the previous analyses, the difference can be attributed to the commission of more heinous homicides and the more serious prior records of the Ohio cohort.

Table 7.7 Parole Performance of Kentucky and Ohio Death Row Inmates Whose Sentences Were Commuted by *Furman v. Georgia*

Variable	Kentucky Cohort	Ohio Cohort
Total Paroled	19 (95%)	20 (43.5%)
Parole Violators		
Hearing Held	3	3
Returned to Prison	2	3
Granted Leniency	1	0
New Crime		
Arrested	4	5
Convicted	4	3
Jailed	1	0
Imprisoned	3	2
Type of Crime		
Robbery	2	0
Burglary	1	0
Theft	0	1
Drug Possession	1	0
Other	0	3
Average Length of the Follow-up Period (in months)	34.4	27.7*
Average Length of Time (in months) Until Recidivism	38.5	32.6*
Arrest Rate	21%	25%
Conviction Rate	21%	15%
Jail Rate	5%	0%
Prison Rate	26%	25%

*Difference between means was not statistically significant.

Despite the difference in the rate of parole between the two groups, they had similar recidivism rates. Nearly all of the parole violators in each group were returned to prison. The rearrest and reconviction rates were similar. None of the paroled inmates in either group committed another murder.

The average length of the follow-up period was longer for the Kentucky cohort as was the average time until recidivism (new offense or violation). Ten of the Ohio parolees were still under and four had cleared supervision at the close of our research. In Kentucky, six parolees had cleared supervision and nine were still on parole during this time frame.

Overall, the recidivism rates of the Ohio cohort are surprisingly like those of their Kentucky counterparts. However, the figures mask the violent offenses committed by two members of the Ohio cohort in prison. One Ohio *Furman* inmate, who was not paroled, killed a correctional officer during a hostage incident in 1973 and was sentenced to life in prison. A second Ohio inmate was paroled in 1981 and returned on a parole violation (weapon possession) in 1982. He subsequently murdered a prison shop supervisor at Lucasville, received a second death sentence, and is presently on Ohio's death row awaiting execution.

CONCLUSION

Overall, the comparisons between the Kentucky and Ohio *Furman* cohorts reveal both similarities and startling differences. The Ohio cohort committed homicides which could be considered more heinous than their Kentucky counterparts. Perhaps, as a result, they had a lower rate of parole and served more time before release than the Kentucky inmates. The Ohio inmates also were more likely to have a stay of execution prior to *Furman*. Thus, they were closer to execution than the Kentucky inmates.

Given their background, the Ohio parolees could be expected to constitute a higher risk to the public. The evidence does not support this contention. While on parole, the performance of the Ohio group is comparable to not only that of the Kentucky parolees but to the *Furman* parolees from other states. According to our survey of the other 25 *Furman* states, 40 percent have been paroled (185/457) and 19.7 percent have been reincarcerated (35/177) (Vito, Koester & Wilson, 1989).

Yet, two Ohio inmates were responsible for two murders of correctional officials after their sentences were commuted. Since this runs counter to the previous findings concerning the institutional behavior of the *Furman* inmates (see Marquart & Sorensen, 1988), these incidents confirm the worst nightmares of correctional personnel regarding the substitution of life without parole for the death penalty. The potential for institutional violence in this cohort may be higher than previously imagined.

In spite of the institutional offenses, the recidivism rates recorded by both groups further emphasize the general conclusion that the execution of these inmates would not have significantly enhanced societal protection. Their recidivism rates were not substantially higher than those of other similarly situated inmates. Our previous chapter indicated that the overall reincarceration rate for all of the *Furman* inmates was approximately 20 percent (Vito, Koester & Wilson, 1989). They did not commit violent crimes in the community. Finally, for all the apparent severity of the Ohio system, their parolees fared no worse than their Southern neighbors. Overall, the experience of the *Furman* cohort demonstrates that the death penalty is not required for societal protection. Supporters of capital punishment must look elsewhere for justifications for society's most severe penalty.

NOTES

One Kentucky inmate died in an accident in a prison boiler room. A second inmate is not eligible for parole since he also was sentenced to life without parole (in addition to death) for rape under the Kentucky code in force at that time (KRS 435.090) (see Vito & Wilson, 1988:103). A third inmate received a stay of execution in 1963 and has been before the parole board several times since his sentence was commuted to life in 1974. At his last hearing, he was given a five-year deferment. Therefore, he will not be eligible for parole until 1992.

REFERENCES

Bowers, W.J. & G.L Pierce (1980). "Arbitrariness and Discrimination Under Post-*Furman* Capital Statutes." *Crime and Delinquency,* 26(October):563-635.

Marquart, J.W. & J.R. Sorensen (1988). "Institutional and Post-Release Behavior of Furman-Commuted Inmates in Texas." *Criminology,* 26(4):677-693.

Vito, G.F., P. Koester & D.G. Wilson (1991). "Return of the Dead: An Update on the Status of *Furman*-Commuted Death Row Inmates." In R.M. Bohm (ed.) *The Death Penalty in America: Current Research.* Cincinnati: Anderson Publishing Co.

Vito, G.F. & T.J. Keil (1988). "Capital Sentencing in Kentucky: An Analysis of the Factors Influencing Decision-Making in the Post-*Gregg* Period." *Journal of Criminal Law and Criminology,* 79(Summer):483-503.

Vito, G.F. & D.G. Wilson (1988). "Back From the Dead: Tracking the Progress of Kentucky's *Furman*-Commuted Death Row Population." *Justice Quarterly,* 5 (March):101-111.

8

American Death Penalty Opinion, 1936-1986: A Critical Examination of the Gallup Polls*

Robert M. Bohm
Department of Criminal Justice
University of North Carolina at Charlotte

INTRODUCTION

Despite more than 50 years of scientific polling and a substantial body of research, an understanding of aggregate American death penalty opinion remains an elusive goal. The purpose of this chapter is to contribute to a greater understanding of the subject by critically examining the 50-year record of American death penalty opinion polls.

An understanding of American death penalty opinion is important, even though most countries that have abolished the death penalty have done so despite relatively strong public support for retention (Zimring & Hawkins, 1986:12). Apart from a heuristic interest in public opinion generally, an understanding of American death penalty opinion is important for a variety of reasons, but especially because greater understanding could very well help to bring an end to the current practice of capital punishment in the United States.

While recent opinion polls clearly show that a majority of Americans support the death penalty in theory, that may be because they are uninformed about the way it is actually administered. Many abolitionists would like to believe that support for the death penalty is a function of a lack of knowledge about it, and that

---

* A version of this chapter was presented at the annual meeting of the American Society of Criminology, Chicago, November, 1988.

opinions are responsive to reasoned persuasion. For example, in *Furman v. Georgia* (408 U.S. 238, 1972), Justice Thurgood Marshall argued that, given information about the death penalty, "the great mass of citizens would conclude...that the death penalty is immoral and therefore unconstitutional" (p. 363; also cf. Sarat & Vidmar, 1976; Vidmar & Dittenhoffer, 1981).

A majority of Americans might reject capital punishment if they knew that the death penalty: (1) does not prevent or reduce crime in general or violent crime in particular more effectively than a noncapital alternative like long imprisonment; (2) causes the executions of innocent persons; (3) is administered (even under post-*Furman* statutes) in a capricious, arbitrary, and odiously discriminatory manner; and (4) as administered, costs much more than life imprisonment—to name only four objections. Rejection might be even greater if the American people realized that the death penalty serves other latent purposes, such as: (1) an instrument of minority group oppression ("to keep blacks in the South in a position of subjugation and subservience"); (2) a tool of majority group protection ("to secure the integrity of the white community in the face of threats or perceived challenges from blacks"); and (3) a repressive response ("to conditions of social dislocation and turmoil in...time of economic hardship") (Bowers, 1984:131-2; Douglas, *Furman v. Georgia,* 408 U.S. 238, 1972; Rusche & Kirchheimer, 1968).

Strong popular demands to abolish the death penalty might be hard for legislators to ignore. Evidence indicates that public opinion has affected policy-making in the United States, as, for example, in the area of civil rights (Oskamp, 1977:241; also cf. Page et al., 1987; Page & Shapiro, 1983; Monroe, 1979; Erikson, 1976; Weissberg, 1976). Furthermore, in the absence of abolition by legislation, public opinion has, and could again, influence abolition of the death penalty in the United States by judicial fiat. A nine-year hiatus on executions (defacto abolition), beginning in June 1967, followed a six-year decline in public support (and an increase in public opposition) that culminated, in 1966, with a plurality of Americans opposed to capital punishment. Both the hiatus on executions and the decline in public support were cited in the *Furman* decision as measures of "evolving community standards" regarding what constitutes "cruel and unusual punishment" under the Eighth Amendment (*Furman v. Georgia,* 408 U.S. 238, 329, 1972; *Gregg v. Georgia,* 428 U.S. 153, 171, 1976; also see *Robinson v. California,* 370 U.S. 660, 666, 1962; *Trop v. Dulles,* 356 U.S. 86, 101, 1958; *Weems v. United States,* 217 U.S. 349, 373, 1910).

However, in light of recent Supreme Court decisions, e.g., *McCleskey v. Kemp,* 107 S. Ct. 1756 (1987), judicial abolition of the death penalty currently appears unlikely. Thus, in the near future, any chance of abolishing the death penalty seems to rest with the American public and its elected representatives. If the death penalty is to be abolished or eroded, a greater understanding of American death penalty opinion may be helpful and necessary.

AMERICAN DEATH PENALTY OPINION, 1936-1986: AN OVERVIEW

Between 1936 and 1986, dozens of national surveys of American death penalty opinion have been conducted, but the longest and most sustained effort belongs to the American Institute of Public Opinion, producers of the Gallup polls.[1] The Gallup organization asked questions about the death penalty in 24 polls between December, 1936 and September, 1987, and information from the original data bases from 21 of those polls forms the basis of this study.[2] Gallup pollsters also have queried respondents about their opinions on the death penalty for many different crimes. This examination, however, is limited to opinions about the death penalty for murder.[3] Finally, although recent Gallup polls have included a greater variety of questions about death penalty opinions, earlier polls focused primarily on percentage distribution of opinions and percentage distribution of opinions by demographic characteristics of respondents. This chapter describes the data contained in most of the polls over the 50-year period, briefly reviews theoretical speculations about the data, and concludes with a discussion of problems with death penalty opinion research generally.

Interviews for the first scientific poll on American death penalty opinion were conducted in December, 1936, shortly after the issue received unprecedented attention by the execution of alleged Lindbergh-baby murderer Bruno Hauptmann.[4] In the poll, 61 percent of respondents answered "yes" that they did "believe in the death penalty for murder" and 39 percent answered "no." The category of "no opinion" or "don't know" was not included as an option (see Table 8.1). The most recent death penalty poll considered in this analysis is the January, 1986 poll, which shows that 70 percent of Americans favor the death penalty, 22 percent are opposed, and 8 percent have no opinion (see Table 8.1).[5]

Note the slight difference in the wording of the questions in the 1936 and 1986 polls. In the former, respondents are asked, "Do you believe in the death penalty for murder?" (In the 1937 poll, respondents were asked, "Do you favor or oppose capital punishment for murder?") In 1986 (and in other polls), respondents are asked, "Do you favor or oppose the death penalty for persons *convicted* of murder?" (emphasis added). While it is unlikely that the addition of the word, "convicted," makes much difference in the distribution of death penalty opinions in these polls, the wording of death penalty questions, as will be discussed in more detail later, can make a significant difference in the distribution of opinions (Bohm & Aveni, 1985; Ellsworth & Ross, 1983; Harris, 1986; Sarat & Vidmar, 1976; Williams, Longmire & Gulick, 1988).

Figure 8.1 displays periods of rising and declining support and opposition of the death penalty between 1936 and 1986.

The overall difference between the two years is a 9 percent increase in support and a 17 percent decrease in opposition. However, using 1937 as a

Table 8.1 American Death Penalty Opinion, 1936-1986: Responses to the Gallup Poll Question about the Death Penalty for Murder (in percentages)

Date of Source Document	Interview Dates	Yes or Favor	No or Oppose	No Opinion or Don't Know
1. 12/7/36	12/2-7/36	61	39	—[a]
2. 12/6/37	12/1-6/37	61	33	7[b]
3. 11/5/53	11/1-5/53	70	29	1[c]
4. 4/3/56	3/29-4/3/56	53	34	13
5. 9/4/57	8/29-9/4/57	47	34	18[d]
6. 3/7/60	3/2-7/60	53	36	11
7. 1/7/65	1/7-12/65	45	43	12
8. 5/24/66	5/19-24/66	42	47	11
9. 6/7/67	6/2-7/67	53	39	8
10. 1/28/69	1/23-28/69	51	40	9
11. 11/2/71	10/29-11/2/71	49	40	11
12. 3/5/72	3/3-5/72	50	42	9
13. 11/13/72	11/10-13/72	57	32	11
14. 11/21/74	10/18-21/74	60	34	6
15. 4/12/76	4/9-12/76	65	28	7
16. 3/6/78	3/3-6/78	62	27	11
17. 2/2/81	1/30-2/2/81	66	25	9
18. 9/20/82	9/17-20/82	72	28	—
19. 1/14/85	1/11-14/85	72	20	8
20. 11/18/85	11/11-18/85	75	17	8
21. 1/13/86	1/10-13/86	70	22	8
	Means	59	33	9

[a]Response category not included.
[b]Gallup (1972) reports 65% favor and 35% oppose.
[c]Gallup (1972) reports 68% yes, 25% no, and 7% no opinion. In this table, response categories "yes/favor" and "yes, qualified" and "no/oppose" and "no, qualified" are combined.
[d]Gallup (1972) reports 47% yes, 50% no, and 3% no opinion.

Source: Original Gallup Poll data bases stored at The Roper Center for Public Opinion Research, Storrs, CT.

reference point, nearly half of the 17 percent decrease in opposition probably would have been recorded as "no opinions" or "don't knows" had that option been provided. In other words, between 1936 and 1986, support for the death penalty increased at the expense of opposition by about 9 percent.

Both Table 8.1 and Figure 8.1 show that the zenith of support was recorded in November, 1985, when 75 percent of Americans favored the death penalty. In that poll, 17 percent were opposed, and 8 percent had no opinion.[6] The nadir in support was 1966, when only 42 percent of respondents voiced support. In that poll, 47 percent were opposed, and 11 percent had no opinion (see Table 8.1 and Figure 8.1).[7] On average, for the twenty-one polls, 59 percent of respondents favored the death penalty, 33 percent opposed it, and 9 percent had "no opinion" or "didn't know" (see Table 8.1).

Although variations in the percentage distributions of death penalty opinions are evident from poll to poll, a close examination of both Table 8.1 and Figure 8.1 reveals two long-term and at least five short-term trends. The watershed year for the long-term trends is 1966, the year that marked the end of a 13-year nonlinear decline and the beginning of a 20-year nonlinear increase in support of the death penalty. Thus, between 1953 and 1966, support of the death penalty decreased 28 percent, opposition increased 18 percent, and "no opinions" or "don't knows" increased 10 percent (see Table 8.1 and Figure 8.1). Between 1966 and 1985, on the other hand, support increased 33 percent, while opposition decreased 30 percent (see Table 8.1 and Figure 8.1).

In the last poll in the sample (March, 1986), the pollsters write that "the trend of public opinion on capital punishment is among the most volatile in Gallup annals" (Gallup, 1987:57). The five, most volatile short-term periods are: (1) 1953-1957 (23% decrease in support, 5% increase in opposition, and 17% increase in "no opinions" or "don't knows"); (2) 1960-1966 (11% decrease in support and 11% increase in opposition); (3) 1966-1967 (11% increase in support and 8% decrease in opposition); (4) 1971-1976 (16% increase in support and 12% decrease in opposition); and (5) 1978-1985 (13% increase in support and 10% decrease in opposition) (see Table 8.1 and Figure 8.1). In a subsequent analysis, a theory of American death penalty opinion will be constructed to explain these trends.

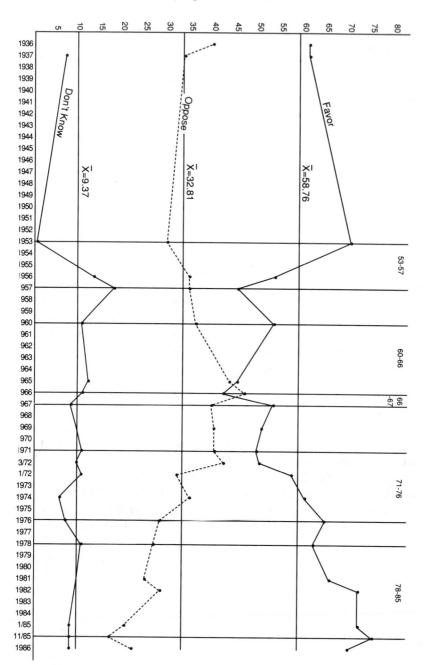

Figure 8.1 American Death Penalty Opinion, 1936-1986.

Comment on "No Opinions" or "Don't Knows"

Over the 50-year period, the percentage of "no opinions" or "don't knows" ranges from 1 percent in 1953 to 18 percent in 1957 with a mean of 9.4 percent. In 1936 and 1982, the category of "no opinion" or "don't know" was not included as a response (see Table 8.1). In an examination of a more limited time period, Smith (1975:265) found an average of 7.9 percent "no opinions" or "don't knows." Smith remarked that this level of uncertainty "is above that found in other general opinion questions, and indicates that people find this a difficult question to take sides on" (1975:265). "No opinions" or "don't knows" are important because of the role they have often played in the swings in death penalty support and opposition over the 50-year period.

DEATH PENALTY OPINION
BY DEMOGRAPHIC CHARACTERISTICS
OF POLL RESPONDENTS

For most of the 21 Gallup polls, information is available on the following ten demographic characteristics: (1) gender, (2) race, (3) age, (4) politics, (5) education, (6) income or SES, (7) occupation, (8) religion, (9) city size, and (10) region of the country. Below is a detailed analysis of the ten demographic characteristics, in order of importance (cf. Vidmar & Ellsworth, 1974 for an earlier summary).

Race

Racial differences are greater than for any other demographic characteristic. In all 21 polls, the percentage of whites who favor the death penalty is greater than the percentage of blacks, while the percentage of blacks opposed and undecided is greater than the percentage of whites (see Table 8.2).

On average, 61 percent of whites have favored the death penalty compared to 41 percent of blacks, and 48 percent of blacks have opposed the death penalty compared to 31 percent of whites (see Table 8.2). In every polling year except 1953 and 1965, the percentage of blacks undecided about the death penalty has surpassed the percentage of whites. About four percent more blacks than whites, on average, have voiced "no opinion" or "don't know" (see Table 8.2).

Racial differences in support or opposition vary greatly over the 50-year period. As indicated above, the mean difference is about 20 percent. The largest differential in support, 32 percent, occurred in both 1976 and 1985, while the smallest, 6 percent, was recorded in 1953. The largest racial differential in opposition, 28 percent, occurred in 1985, while the smallest, 5 percent, was registered in both 1937 and 1957 (see Table 8.2).

For whites, the highpoint in support and lowpoint in opposition was November, 1985, when 78 percent indicated support and only 15 percent registered opposition. The lowpoint in support and highpoint in opposition for whites was 1966, when 44 percent supported the death penalty and 46 percent opposed it. In only 1965 and 1966 has less than 50 percent of whites supported the death

Table 8.2 American Death Penalty Opinion, 1936-1986: Responses to the Gallup Poll Question about the Death Penalty for Murder by Race, in percentages (F = Favored; O = Opposed; U = Undecided)

Date of Source Document	Whites			Blacks		
	F	**O**	**U**	**F**	**O**	**U**
1. 12/7/36	61	39	—	38	63	—[a]
2. 12/6/37	61	33	6	47	38	15
3. 11/5/53	71	29	1	65	35	0
4. 4/3/56	55	33	13	42	44	14
5. 9/4/57	48	34	18	41	39	20
6. 3/7/60	55	35	10	38	45	17
7. 1/7/65	46	42	12	35	56	10
8. 5/24/66	44	46	8	22	59	20
9. 6/7/67	55	37	7	39	48	14
10. 1/28/69	53	39	8	29	57	14
11. 11/2/71	51	38	11	30	58	12
12. 3/5/72	53	39	8	24	64	12
13. 11/13/72	60	29	11	32	52	16
14. 10/21/74	62	32	5	42	49	9
15. 4/12/76	70	24	6	38	51	11
16. 3/6/78	64	26	10	41	44	14
17. 2/2/81	70	22	8	44	44	12
18. 9/20/82	75	25	—	55	45	—
19. 1/14/85	75	18	6	57	35	8
20. 11/18/85	78	15	7	46	43	11
21. 1/13/86	73	19	8	47	43	10
Means	61	31	9	41	48	13

[a]Response category not included.

Source: See Table 8.1.

penalty. As for blacks, the highpoint in support was 1953, when 65 percent expressed support; the lowpoint was in 1966 when only 22 percent did so. The high-point in opposition for blacks came in 1972, when 64 percent of blacks opposed the death penalty; the lowpoint was in both 1953 and 1985, when 35 percent were opposed. In only 3 of the 21 polling years, 1953, 1982, and January, 1985, have a majority of blacks favored the death penalty. However, in 13 of the 21 poll years, a majority of blacks did not oppose the death penalty either, which is mostly attributable to the large percentages of blacks who have been undecided about the death penalty. The percentage of blacks undecided has varied between 0 percent in 1953 and 20 percent in 1957 and 1966, while the percentage of whites undecided has varied between 1 percent in 1953 and 18 percent in 1957 (see Table 8.2).

Smith (1975:269) suggests that racial differences in support and opposition of the death penalty can be attributed to "the disproportionate application of the death penalty to blacks" and to "the civil rights movement, which increased black sensitivity to such inequalities." That may be true for the 1953-1966 and 1960-1966 periods where a 16 and 5 percent greater decrease in support and a 7 and 3 percent greater increase in opposition were recorded for blacks than for whites, but it does not seem to apply as neatly to the other periods. Between 1966 and 1985, for example, black support of the death penalty increased by 24 per-cent, just 10 percent less than the increase by whites. White opposition, on the other hand, declined 31 percent between 1966 and 1985, while black opposition declined only 16 percent. In the 1966-1967 period, during the heart of the civil rights movement, black support of the death penalty increased 6 percent more than white support. Despite these disparities, white and black support and opposi-tion have always increased and decreased in the same directions.

Income or SES

Data for income or socioeconomic status (SES) is available for 19 of the 21 polls (see Table 8.3). In every year for which there are data, people in the top income or socioeconomic category have been more likely to support the death penalty and less likely to oppose it than people in the bottom category.[8] In nearly every year except 1936, differences have been substantial. On average, 64 percent of people in the top income category have favored the death penalty compared to

50 percent of people in the bottom income category. As for opposition, an average of 30 percent of people in the top income category have opposed the death penalty compared to 39 percent of people in the bottom income category. Thus, the mean difference between the top and bottom income categories for support of the death penalty is 14 percent, while the mean difference for opposition is 9 percent. In every poll for which there is data, except 1965 and 1976, the percentage of undecideds in the bottom category has exceeded the percentage in the top category by an average of about 6 percent (see Table 8.3).

Table 8.3 American Death Penalty Opinion, 1936-1986: Responses to the Gallup Poll Question about the Death Penalty for Murder by Income or SES, in percentages (F = Favored; O = Opposed; U = Undecided)

Date of Source Document	Top Category			Middle Category			Bottom Category		
	F	O	U	F	O	U	F	O	U
1. 12/7/36	64	36	—	61	39	—	60	40	—
2. 12/6/37	70	26	5	61	33	6	58	34	8
3. 4/3/56	62	28	10	52	32	16	48	40	13
4. 9/4/57	54	32	14	47	33	20	41	39	20
5. 1/7/65*	48	39	13	—	—	—	39	50	11
6. 5/24/66*	45	47	8	—	—	—	40	50	10
7. 6/7/67*	60	37	3	—	—	—	48	43	10
8. 1/28/69*	55	38	7	—	—	—	47	40	13
9. 11/2/71*	54	37	9	—	—	—	40	42	18
10. 3/5/72*	52	41	7	—	—	—	43	43	14
11. 11/13/72*	61	32	7	—	—	—	38	43	19
12. 10/21/74	61	33	6	65	32	3	50	42	8
13. 4/12/76	72	24	4	69	22	9	52	46	2
14. 3/6/78	65	26	9	63	25	11	46	34	21
15. 2/2/81*	74	21	5	—	—	—	52	34	14
16. 9/20/82*	78	22	—	—	—	—	59	41	—
17. 1/14/85	80	17	3	75	16	9	63	26	11
18. 11/18/85*	77	19	4	—	—	—	67	25	8
19. 1/13/86*	79	17	4	—	—	—	60	27	13
Means	64	30	7	62	29	11	50	39	13

*See footnote 8.

Source: See Table 8.1.

For the top income category, support for the death penalty has ranged from a low of 45 percent in 1966 to a high of 80 percent in January, 1985 (see Table 8.3). Opposition for this group has ranged from a high of 47 percent in 1966 to a low of 17 percent in both January, 1985 and 1986. For the bottom income category, on the other hand, support has ranged from a low of 38 percent in November, 1972 to a high of 67 percent in November, 1985. Opposition for the bottom income category has ranged from a high of 50 percent in both 1965 and 1966 to a low of 25 percent in November, 1985 (see Table 8.3).

Smith (1975:269) reported data on income differentials from eight national death penalty opinion polls conducted between 1965 and 1974 and remarked that "there has been a constant relationship between low income and opposition to the death penalty." Smith attributes these differences to "a greater interest in order by the economically secure groups," as well as "a belief among the poorer group of class inequities in the judicial [sic] system in general, and the punishment of capital crimes in particular" (1975:269, 278). Combs and Comer (1982) found that for whites, increased income is related to both a shift toward conservative ideology and support for the death penalty. Furthermore, when income was introduced as a control variable, Smith (1975:278) discovered that relationships found between educational differences and death penalty opinions were spurious (see Education below).

Gender

In all 21 polls, the percentage of males who favor the death penalty exceeds the percentage of females, and the percentage of females opposed to the death penalty exceeds the percentage of males (see Table 8.4). On average, 65 percent of males have favored the death penalty compared to 53 percent of females, while 29 percent of males and 37 percent of females have opposed it. Except for November, 1985, when percentages were the same, the percentage of females undecided about the death penalty has always surpassed the percentage of males. About four percent more females than males, on average, have had "no opinion" or "don't know" (see Table 8.4).

The highpoint in support of the death penalty for both males and females was November 1985, when 78 percent of males and 73 percent of females voiced support. The lowpoint in support for males, 47 percent, came in 1966, which, incidentally, is the only year where less than 50 percent of males favored the death penalty (see Table 8.4). The lowpoint in support for females was 1965, when 37 percent expressed support. In ten of the 21 polling years, but in none after 1972, less than 50 percent of females favored the death penalty (see Table 8.4). The highpoint

Table 8.4 American Death Penalty Opinion, 1936-1986: Responses to the Gallup Poll Question about the Death Penalty for Murder by Gender, in percentages (F = Favored; O = Opposed; U = Undecided)

Date of Source Document	Male			Female		
	F	**O**	**U**	**F**	**O**	**U**
1. 12/7/36	65	35	—	49	51	—a
2. 12/6/37	65	29	6	51	41	8
3. 11/5/53	75	25	*b	66	33	1
4. 4/3/56	59	29	11	48	38	14
5. 9/4/57	53	33	14	42	36	22
6. 3/7/60	58	33	9	48	39	13
7. 1/7/65	54	37	9	37	49	14
8. 5/24/66	47	45	8	38	49	13
9. 6/7/67	61	33	7	48	43	9
10. 1/28/69	60	34	6	44	45	11
11. 11/2/71	56	36	8	43	44	13
12. 3/5/72	55	39	6	45	43	12
13. 11/13/72	64	26	10	50	37	13
14. 10/21/74	66	30	4	55	38	7
15. 4/12/76	69	25	6	63	30	7
16. 3/6/78	70	22	8	55	32	13
17. 2/2/81	71	22	7	62	28	10
18. 9/20/82	76	24	—	69	31	—
19. 1/14/85	78	16	6	67	24	9
20. 11/18/85	78	15	7	73	20	7
21. 1/13/86	74	19	7	66	24	10
Means	65	29	8	53	37	11

aResponse category not included.
bLess than .05.

Source: See Table 8.1.

in opposition for males was 45 percent in 1966 and 51 percent for females in 1936. The latter year, 1936, is the only year in which over 50 percent of females opposed the death penalty (see Table 8.4). The lowpoint in opposition for both males and females came in 1985, when 15 percent of males and 20 percent of females opposed the death penalty (see Table 8.4).

Gender differences in death penalty support and opposition have been attributed to differences in the socialization processes of boys and girls (cf., Gelles & Straus, 1976; Perkes & Schildt, 1979; Smith, 1975; Vidmar & Miller, 1980). What is curious and what requires explanation is that, despite variation between genders over time, each gender has followed the aggregate trend.

Politics

Table 8.5 displays data on death penalty opinion by politics for 19 of the 21 polls (political party data are not available for 1936 and 1937). An examination of the 19 polls reveals that, in general, Democrats have shown the greatest opposition and the least support for the death penalty; Independents are less opposed and more supportive; and Republicans are least opposed and most supportive (see Table 8.5). On average, 65 percent of Republicans, 58 percent of Independents, and 55 percent of Democrats have supported the death penalty, while 36 percent of Democrats, 34 percent of Independents, and 27 percent of Republicans have opposed it. The average percentage of "no opinions" or "don't knows" for each party has fallen in the 9 percent range (see Table 8.5).

Differences in support or opposition to the death penalty by politics have varied substantially between 1953 and 1986. The mean difference is about 10 percent. The largest difference in support between Democrats and Republicans is 20 percent in 1986, while the smallest difference is 2 percent recorded in 1957. The largest difference in opposition, 19 percent, occurred in 1986, while the smallest difference, 2 percent, was registered in 1957 (see Table 8.5).

For Democrats, the highpoint in support, 70 percent, came in 1982, while the lowpoint in support, 39 percent, was achieved in 1966. The highpoint in opposition, 51 percent, occurred in 1966, while the lowpoint in opposition, 25 percent, was in 1985 (see Table 8.5). In five of the 19 polling years, 1957, 1965, 1966, 1971, and March, 1972, Democratic support of the death penalty fell below

Table 8.5 American Death Penalty Opinion, 1936-1986: Responses to the Gallup Poll Question about the Death Penalty for Murder by Politics, in percentages
(F = Favored; O = Opposed; U = Undecided)

Date of Source Document	Democrats			Republicans			Independents		
	F	O	U	F	O	U	F	O	U
1. 11/5/53	68	30	1	73	26	1	71	30	0
2. 4/3/56	51	36	13	59	30	11	49	34	16
3. 9/4/57	46	35	19	48	33	19	48	38	15
4. 3/7/60	51	39	10	55	33	12	54	34	11
5. 1/7/65	42	46	12	49	40	11	47	43	10
6. 5/24/66	39	51	10	51	40	9	41	48	11
7. 6/7/67	51	41	8	59	35	5	54	37	9
8. 1/28/69	50	40	10	55	36	9	50	43	7
9. 11/2/71	44	44	12	53	37	10	41	45	14
10. 3/5/72	49	44	7	59	29	12	44	48	8
11. 11/13/72	51	37	12	62	29	9	59	30	11
12. 10/21/74	58	37	5	69	27	5	59	37	5
13. 4/12/76	62	31	7	75	18	7	66	29	5
14. 3/6/78	59	29	12	72	20	8	61	30	9
15. 2/2/81	64	27	9	73	19	8	65	27	8
16. 9/20/82	70	30	—	79	21	—	70	30	—
17. 1/14/85	65	25	10	82	13	5	71	21	8
18. 11/18/85	66	25	9	84	10	6	76	17	7
19. 1/13/86	62	30	8	82	11	6	69	22	9
Means	55	36	10	65	27	9	58	34	9

Source: See Table 8.1.

50 percent. However, in only the one polling year, 1966, did a majority of Democrats oppose the death penalty (see Table 8.5). Incidentally, summary material for the 1974 poll reveals that Southern Democrats were a little more likely to support the death penalty than were other Democrats (65% to 59%).

For Republicans, the highpoint in support of the death penalty, 84 percent, came in 1985, while the lowpoint, 48 percent, was recorded in 1957. The highpoint in opposition, 40 percent, was registered in both 1965 and 1966, while the lowpoint in opposition, 10 percent, occurred in 1985 (see Table 8.5). In only two years, 1957 and 1965, have less than a majority of Republicans favored the death penalty, and in no polling year has a majority of Republicans opposed the death penalty (see Table 8.5).

Finally, the highpoint in support of the death penalty for Independents came in 1985, when 76 percent supported the death penalty. The lowpoint in support, 41 percent, was recorded in both 1966 and 1971. The highpoint in opposition for Independents, 48 percent, was registered in both 1966 and March, 1972, while the lowpoint in opposition, 17 percent, occurred in 1985 (see Table 8.5). In six years, 1956, 1957, 1965, 1966, 1971, and March, 1972, less than a majority of Independents favored the death penalty. However, in no polling year has a majority of Independents opposed the death penalty (see Table 8.5).

Region of the country

Information on region of the country is available for 20 of the 21 polls. Though some variation occurs from year-to-year, overall, the South, surprisingly, has been the region least likely to support and most likely to oppose the death penalty (means = 55 and 36%, respectively) (see Table 8.6). Following the South, in order of least support and greatest opposition are the Midwest (means = 58 and 34%), the East (means = 61 and 31%), and the West (means = 64 and 29%). As for "undecideds," the West has averaged about 7 percent; the Midwest, 9 percent; the East, 9 percent; and the South, 10 percent (see Table 8.6).

The mean difference between the South, which has shown, on average, the least support and greatest opposition, and the West, which has demonstrated the opposite, is about 9 percent for support and 7 percent for opposition. Greatest support by any region is the 78 percent recorded for the West in November, 1985. (In that poll, 75% of respondents in the East and 74% in the Midwest and South expressed support.) (See Table 8.6.) Least support by any region is the 35 percent recorded for the South in 1966. The least support in the East is 45 percent in 1966; in the Midwest, 39 percent in 1965; and in the West, 44 percent in 1957 (see Table 8.6). The years in which less than 50 percent of respondents by region supported the death penalty are 1966 and 1971 for the East; 1957, 1960, 1965, 1966, 1971, and 1972 for the Midwest; 1956, 1957, 1960, 1965, 1966, 1967, 1969, 1971, and 1972 for the South; and 1957 for the West (see Table 8.6).

Table 8.6 American Death Penalty Opinion, 1936-1986: Responses to the Gallup Poll Question about the Death Penalty for Murder by Region, in percentages (F = Favored; O = Opposed; U = Undecided)

Date of Source Document	East			Midwest			South			West		
	F	O	U	F	O	U	F	O	U	F	O	U
1. 12/7/36	59	38	3	54	43	2	61	35	4	59	39	3
2. 12/6/37	63	32	5	57	36	7	60	31	9	67	27	6
3. 11/5/53	75	24	—	67	32	1	65	34	1	74	23	2
4. 4/3/56	54	32	14	55	32	13	46	39	15	62	31	7
5. 9/4/57	57	25	18	47	34	19	37	44	19	44	39	17
6. 3/7/60	61	28	11	45	43	12	46	41	14	59	33	8
7. 1/7/65	54	34	12	39	51	10	36	50	14	56	34	10
8. 5/24/66	45	43	12	42	48	10	35	53	12	50	42	8
9. 6/7/67	57	35	8	54	39	8	41	50	10	64	31	4
10. 1/28/69	51	39	10	51	43	6	46	45	9	63	28	9
11. 11/2/71	49	38	13	48	43	9	47	42	11	54	38	8
12. 3/5/72	55	34	11	42	49	9	46	46	8	59	33	8
13. 10/21/74	59	34	6	60	36	4	61	31	7	59	35	5
14. 4/12/76	65	28	7	70	22	8	59	35	6	70	25	5
15. 3/6/78	65	26	9	67	24	9	56	30	14	59	31	10
16. 2/2/81	67	24	9	65	25	10	65	26	9	70	25	5
17. 9/20/82	75	25	—	75	25	—	65	35	—	75	25	—
18. 1/14/85	66	25	9	73	19	8	74	19	7	77	16	7
19. 11/18/85	75	21	4	74	19	7	74	17	9	78	12	10
21. 1/13/86	64	26	10	73	17	10	69	23	8	76	20	4
Means	61	31	9	58	34	9	55	36	10	64	29	7

Source: See Table 8.1.

Greatest opposition is the 53 percent recorded for the South in 1966. Greatest opposition in the East is the 43 percent in 1966; in the Midwest, the 51 percent in 1965; and in the West, the 42 percent in 1966. Only in the South in 1966 and in the Midwest in 1965 have over 50 percent of respondents opposed the death penalty, though 50 percent of respondents in the South were opposed in 1965 and 1967 (see Table 8.6). Least opposition is the 12 percent in the West in November, 1985. Least opposition in the East is the 21 percent in November, 1985; in the Midwest the 17 percent in 1986; and in the South the 17 percent in November, 1985 (see Table 8.6).

Perhaps the most perplexing anomaly of this examination is that, in 13 of the 20 polls, the South compared to the other three regions has voiced or has tied for voicing the least support for the death penalty. (The years are 1953, 1956, 1957, 1965, 1966, 1967, 1969, 1971, 1976, 1978, 1981, 1982, and November, 1985.) Looked at differently, in 9 of the 20 polls, the South has expressed the greatest opposition to the death penalty of any of the four regions. (The years are 1953, 1956, 1957, 1966, 1967, 1969, 1976, 1981, and 1982.) The only year in which the South has expressed the most support for the death penalty is 1936, though in that year differences between regions were negligible. The puzzle is how to reconcile the findings about opinion with the fact that, since 1930, the South has led the nation in executions. Indeed, between 1930 and 1980, 60 percent of all executions have occurred in the South—3.75 times more executions than in any other region of the United States (see Bedau, 1982:56-57). Furthermore, under post-*Furman* statutes (those enacted after 1972), 93 percent of executions have occurred in the South (*Death Row, U.S.A.*, 1988). Two possible and interrelated explanations for the anomaly are (1) the disproportionate percentages of blacks and the poor in the South (both groups are less likely to support the death penalty), along with an almost totally white gentry judiciary (both groups are more likely to support the death penalty), and (2) the well-supported psychological finding that expressed opinions often differ dramatically from actual practice.

Age

Information on age is available for 20 of the 21 polls. Only data for age in the 1936 poll is missing. Until 1960, people under 30 were more likely to favor and less likely to oppose the death penalty than people 50 and over.[9] People 30-49 usually fell somewhere in between (see Table 8.7). After 1960, the trend reversed and, since then, people over 50 have been more likely to support and less likely to oppose the death penalty than people under 30. Of late, opinions of people 30-49 have generally been closer to the 50 and over group than those 30 and under. People under 30 are less likely to be undecided (8%) than people 30-49 (9%), or people 50 and over (11%) (see Table 8.7).

Means for the 20 polls show that approximately 60 percent of all age groups have favored the death penalty, while between 30-36 percent have opposed it (see Table 8.7). In the 1986 poll, age differences were negligible, as approximately 70 percent of all age groups favored the death penalty. (Differences in opposition and undecideds were more substantial.) (see Table 8.7). The least support and greatest opposition for all three groups were registered in 1966. For the under-30 group, 40 percent supported and 50 percent opposed the death penalty; for the 30-49 group, the corresponding figures are 43 and 45 percent; and for the 50 and over group, the percentages are 43 and 47 (see Table 8.7). The most support and least opposition were recorded in January, 1985 for the under-30 group (74 and 20%) and in November, 1985 for both the 30-49 group (76 and 18%) and the 50 and over group (80 and 12%) (see Table 8.7). The only year in which a majority of any age group opposed the death penalty was 1972 (March), when 52 percent of the under-30 group was opposed (see Table 8.7).[10]

Table 8.7 American Death Penalty Opinion, 1936-1986: Responses to the Gallup Poll Question about the Death Penalty for Murder by Age, in percentages (F = Favored; O = Opposed; U = Undecided)

Date of Source Document	Under 30			30-49			50 and over		
	F	O	U	F	O	U	F	O	U
1. 12/6/37	64	31	5	60	33	7	58	34	8
2. 11/5/53[a]	72	26	1	71	28	0	67	32	1
3. 4/3/56	59	28	13	54	32	14	50	38	12
4. 9/4/57	50	31	19	48	34	18	46	36	18
5. 3/7/60	53	40	7	55	34	12	51	37	12
6. 1/7/65	44	48	8	44	44	12	46	41	13
7. 5/24/66	40	50	10	43	45	12	43	47	10
8. 6/7/67	47	47	7	54	39	7	55	36	9
9. 1/28/69	47	46	7	53	39	8	52	38	10
10. 11/2/71[b]	48	43	9	50	40	10	50	36	14
11. 3/5/72	42	52	6	52	40	8	54	34	12
12. 11/13/72*	55	35	10	58	31	11	60	27	13
13. 10/24/74	51	47	2	62	31	6	65	27	8
14. 4/12/76*	60	32	8	70	25	5	67	25	8
15. 3/6/78	57	35	8	64	26	10	65	22	13
16. 2/2/81*	62	31	7	68	24	8	68	22	10
17. 9/20/82*	72	28	—	73	27	—	73	27	—[c]
18. 1/14/85*	74	20	6	73	20	7	73	17	10
19. 11/18/85*	65	24	11	76	18	6	80	12	8
20. 1/13/86*	68	28	4	72	21	7	69	20	11
Means	57	36	8	60	32	9	60	30	11

[a]Response categories "yes/favor" and "yes, qualified" are combined, as are "no/oppose" and "no/qualified."

[b]"Under 30" category = 21-29 years of age. Response category, "18-20" is not included. Percentages for 1971 for 18- to 20-year-olds is: F = 40; O = 54; U = 6.

[c]"No opinion" or "Don't know" category not included.

*"Under 30" category = 25-29 years of age. Response category, "18-24," is not included. Percentages for 18 to 24 age category (F/O/U) are: 1972 (48/44/8); 1976 (57/38/5); 1981 (63/30/7); 1982 (70/30/—); 1/1985 (69/27/4); 11/1985 (72/22/6); 1986 (71/21/8).

Source: See Table 8.1.

Education

Data on education is available for 19 of the 21 polls. In all but three of the 19 polls (1965, 1966, and 1969) education appears to influence death penalty opinions (see Table 8.8). In recent years, high school graduates are most likely, or as likely, to favor the death penalty than are graduates of other levels (this was true in the November, 1972, 1976, 1978, 1981, 1982, January, 1985, November, 1985, and 1986 polls) (see Table 8.8). Grade school graduates are least likely to favor the death penalty, though in some polls percentages approach the levels of other educational levels (e.g., the 1982 poll). Finally, college graduates were more likely to favor the death penalty than the other educational levels in the 1953 and 1956 polls, but since then, have approached the high level of support by high school graduates in only the November, 1972 and January, 1985 polls (see Table 8.8).

Table 8.8 American Death Penalty Opinion, 1936-1986: Responses to the Gallup Poll Question about the Death Penalty for Murder by Education, in percentages (F = Favored; O = Opposed; U = Undecided)

Date of Source Document	College			High School			Grade School		
	F	O	U	F	O	U	F	O	U
1. 11/5/53	77	22	0	68	30	1	72	28	0
2. 4/3/56	64	29	7	55	33	12	48	36	16
3. 9/4/57	50	40	10	48	34	18	46	32	22
4. 3/7/60	47	46	7	54	35	11	53	34	13
5. 1/7/65	43	48	9	48	41	11	43	44	13
6. 5/24/66	46	46	8	41	48	11	42	46	12
7. 6/7/67	50	47	3	55	37	8	51	38	10
8. 1/28/69	52	43	5	52	38	10	48	42	10
9. 11/2/71	50	45	5	50	39	11	45	39	16
10. 3/5/72	48	47	5	51	39	10	50	40	10
11. 11/13/72	57	36	7	60	29	11	49	34	17
12. 10/21/74	56	40	4	62	33	5	61	30	10
13. 4/12/76	62	33	5	69	24	7	62	30	8
14. 3/6/78	61	32	8	66	25	10	53	29	18
15. 2/2/81	62	32	6	72	20	8	55	30	15
16. 9/20/82	67	33	—	75	25	—	72	28	—
17. 1/14/85	74	22	4	75	19	6	65	23	12
18. 11/18/85	71	22	7	79	15	6	72	15	13
19. 1/13/86	67	26	7	75	19	6	63	23	14
Means	58	36	6	61	31	9	55	33	13

Source: See Table 8.1.

Conversely, college graduates have been more likely to oppose the death penalty than graduates of either high school or grade school. Except for the 1953 and 1956 polls, this has been true for every poll in which differences are significant (see Table 8.8). In the November, 1972 and 1981 polls, opposition by grade school graduates was almost as great as opposition by college graduates (see Table 8.8).

Means for support of the death penalty are 55 percent for grade school graduates, 61 percent for high school graduates, and 58 percent for college graduates (see Table 8.8). Means for opposition, on the other hand, are 33 percent for grade school graduates, 31 percent for high school graduates, and 36 percent for college graduates (see Table 8.8). In no polling year has a majority of respondents in any education category opposed the death penalty. Means for respondents undecided are approximately 13 percent for grade school graduates, 9 percent for high school graduates, and 6 percent for college graduates (see Table 8.8). As might be expected, education seems to reduce uncertainty about the death penalty.

Nevertheless, recall that Smith discovered that relationships between educational differences and death penalty opinions were spurious. As Smith (1975:278) explains, "income was creating a spurious difference between the less-educated and high school graduates, while supressing the relationship between the college-educated and high school graduates, and between the middle and wealthy groups and the less well off." Empirical corroboration of Smith's finding, unfortunately, must await future research.

Occupation

Twenty of the 21 polls contain data on occupation. Though several different occupational categories are provided in different polls, three categories, "professional and business," "clerical/sales," and "manual," are found in most of the polls. In general, death penalty support and opposition do not vary greatly between the three occupational categories. Means for support are 58 percent for professional and business and manual and 64 percent for clerical/sales (see Table 8.9). Means for opposition are 28 percent for clerical/sales, 33 percent for manual, and 35 percent for professional and business (see Table 8.9). In no polling year has a majority of any occupational category opposed the death penalty, though in 1966, 50 percent of manual workers were opposed (see Table 8.9). Means for undecideds are approximately 9 percent for manual and clerical/sales and 7 percent for professional and business (see Table 8.9).

Table 8.9 American Death Penalty Opinion, 1936-1986: Responses to the Gallup Poll Question about the Death Penalty for Murder by Occupation, in percentages (F = Favored; O = Opposed; U = Undecided)

Date of Source Document	Prof. and Bus.			Clerical/Sales			Manual		
	F	O	U	F	O	U	F	O	U
1. 12/7/36	62	36	2	—	—	—	—	—	—
2. 12/6/37	64	32	4	—	—	—	—	—	—
3. 11/5/53	72	28	0	68	31	2	70	30	0
4. 4/3/56	58	31	11	52	35	14	54	33	13
5. 9/4/57	47	38	15	54	28	18	49	33	18
6. 3/7/60	52	39	9	49	41	10	55	33	12
7. 1/7/65	44	46	10	—	—	—	47	41	12
8. 5/24/66	43	48	9	—	—	—	40	50	10
9. 6/7/67	52	43	4	52	39	9	53	39	8
10. 1/28/69	48	44	8	—	—	—	51	41	8
11. 11/2/71	48	44	8	—	—	—	49	41	10
12. 3/5/72	51	44	5	—	—	—	48	43	9
13. 11/13/72	55	34	11	66	25	9	59	31	10
14. 10/21/74	59	36	4	59	34	7	61	35	5
15. 4/12/76	64	32	4	67	23	10	66	27	7
16. 3/6/78	63	29	8	63	30	7	62	27	11
17. 2/2/81	66	27	7	68	24	8	68	25	7
18. 9/20/82	73	27	—	76	24	—	75	25	—
19. 1/14/85	74	21	5	78	15	7	72	20	8
20. 1/13/86	72	21	7	78	16	6	69	24	7
Means	58	35	7	64	28	9	58	33	9

Source: See Table 8.1.

Religion

In 17 of the 21 polls, data are provided on the death penalty opinions of Protestants and Catholics. With the exception of 1965, when ten percent more Catholics than Protestants favored the death penalty (perhaps in response to the assassination of President Kennedy, a Catholic), no major differences in support or opposition between Catholics and Protestants are evident. On average, 59 and 62 percent of Protestants and Catholics, respectively, have favored the death penalty and 33 percent of Protestants and 30 percent of Catholics have opposed it. For both groups, approximately 8 percent of respondents have been undecided (see Table 8.10).

Table 8.10 American Death Penalty Opinion, 1936-1986: Responses to the Gallup Poll Question about the Death Penalty for Murder by Religion, in percentages (F = Favored; O = Opposed; U = Undecided)

Date of Source Document	Protestants			Catholics		
	F	O	U	F	O	U
1. 11/5/53	68	30	1	75	24	1
2. 3/7/60	51	38	11	54	36	10
3. 1/7/65	42	45	13	52	38	10
4. 5/24/66	42	48	10	44	45	11
5. 6/7/67	52	41	7	57	34	9
6. 1/28/69	51	40	9	54	37	9
7. 11/2/71	50	38	12	50	42	8
8. 3/5/72	49	42	9	52	38	10
9. 11/13/72	57	32	11	60	29	11
10. 10/21/74	61	33	6	65	31	4
11. 4/12/76	65	28	7	70	24	6
12. 3/6/78	62	27	11	65	25	10
13. 2/2/81	65	26	9	70	22	8
14. 9/20/82	72	28	—	75	25	—[a]
15. 1/14/85	74	19	7	71	20	9
16. 11/18/85	76	18	6	76	16	8
17. 1/13/86	72	20	8	70	22	8
Means	59	32	9	62	30	8

[a]Response category not included.

Source: See Table 8.1.

City Size

Data on city size are available for 16 of the 21 polls. Though differences in support and opposition are discernible, clear-cut trends are not. Means for support of the death penalty are between 55 and 61 percent, for opposition between 31 and 36 percent, and for undecideds between 8 and 11 percent (see Table 8.11). Note that people in cities of 1,000,000 and over, for which data are available in only 12 polls, are a little more likely to support and a little less likely to oppose the death penalty than people in cities of other sizes (see Table 8.11).

Table 8.11 American Death Penalty Opinion, 1936-1986: Responses to the Gallup Poll Question about the Death Penalty for Murder by City Size, in percentages (F = Favored; O = Opposed; U = Undecided)

Date of Source Document	1,000,000 & over			500,000-999,999			2,500-499,999			49,999			under 2,500		
	F	O	U	F	O	U	F	O	U	F	O	U	F	O	U
1. 11/5/53	—	—	—	75	26	0	66	31	1	73	26	0	68	33	1
2. 4/3/56	55	32	13	59	29	12	55	32	13	53	34	13	51	36	13
3. 9/4/57	58	25	17	47	32	21	46	40	14	43	33	25	45	38	17
4. 3/7/60	50	36	13	56	30	14	55	36	10	50	40	10	53	37	10
5. 1/7/65	—	—	—	50	40	10	42	46	12	47	39	14	41	47	12
6. 5/24/66	—	—	—	43	43	14	43	49	8	47	44	9	39	51	10
7. 6/7/67	58	34	10	57	42	1	51	43	6	56	37	6	49	39	11
8. 1/28/69	—	—	—	54	39	7	57	36	7	47	44	9	46	42	12
9. 11/2/71	55	35	10	46	43	11	43	47	10	48	42	10	51	37	12
10. 3/5/72	58	35	7	46	44	10	45	45	10	48	43	9	51	40	9
11. 11/13/72	54	34	12	59	31	10	59	28	13	52	38	10	58	32	10
12. 10/21/74	62	31	7	55	40	5	59	36	6	63	34	3	61	32	7
13. 4/12/76	68	25	7	65	30	5	64	30	6	64	28	8	67	26	7
14. 3/6/78	69	20	11	58	34	9	63	27	10	57	34	9	62	24	13
15. 2/2/81	67	23	10	62	30	8	69	25	6	65	28	7	67	21	12
16. 9/20/82	75	25	—	69	31	—	68	32	—	75	25	—	74	26	—
Means	61	30	11	56	35	9	55	36	9	56	36	8	55	35	10

Source: See Table 8.1.

Summary

The preceding examination reveals that mean percentage differences between the attributes of five of the ten demographic characteristics vary substantially over the 50-year period, while mean differences between the attributes of the five other characteristics do not. Greatest mean differences, in order of the magnitude of that difference, were found for race, income or SES, gender, politics, and region of the country. In other words, between 1936 and 1986, whites, wealthier people, males, Republicans, and Westerners have tended to support the death penalty more than blacks, poorer people, females, Democrats, and Southerners. The characteristics with much less variation over the 50 years are age, education, occupation, religion, and city size.

In the 1986 poll, the most recent one considered here, a majority of people in all demographic categories except race supported the death penalty. However, within categories, substantial variation was found for all of the demographic characteristics except religion. City size was not a category in the 1986 poll. Thus, blacks, females, people under 30, Democrats, college graduates, people in the bottom income or SES category, manual laborers, and Easterners and Southerners were less likely to support or more likely to oppose the death penalty than whites, males, Republicans, high school graduates, people in the top income category, clerical and sales workers, and Westerners and Midwesterners.

Social demographic differences, as interesting and important as they are for an understanding of aggregate American death penalty opinion, are not enough. Also important is an explanation of variations in demographic characteristics over time. For that, historical analysis is indispensable. Over the two long-term and five short-term periods of greatest variation, with minor and inconsequential exceptions, increases and decreases in support and opposition for all ten demographic characteristics followed the aggregate trend. This finding suggests that variations in aggregate death penalty opinions over time are best explained by social events. A social history of American death penalty opinion is the object of future research. However, before beginning such a project, and to allow for a more critical interpretation of the findings presented in this chapter, the next section considers some of the problems with data in death penalty opinion research.

PROBLEMS WITH DATA ON AMERICAN DEATH PENALTY OPINION

Theory-building using opinion poll and other survey data must be tempered by a critical appreciation of their limitations. Problems with all social survey research are sampling and measurement errors. Results, in other words, may be the product of peculiarities of the sample selected or with the way data are collected, and not an accurate representation of the American population. While these problems can never be dismissed lightly, because of increasingly sophisticated sampling techniques and the enviable track record of the Gallup organization in predicting political outcomes from its polls, sampling and measurement errors likely had little effect on the data in this study, particularly in the later polls. Sampling error (i.e., the error introduced because samples vary from one to the next) probably did not exceed 3 to 3.5% in any of the Gallup polls discussed in this study (from conversation with Marc Maynard of The Roper Center).

A fundamental problem with all death penalty opinion research is uncertainty about what death penalty support or opposition actually means. First, most Americans are not well-informed about the death penalty and its effects (Bohm & Aveni, 1985; Ellsworth & Ross, 1983; Sarat & Vidmar, 1976). Thus, what little we know about American death penalty opinion is based on responses of people who know very little about it. The ignorance of most Americans about the death penalty indicates that, generally, death penalty opinions are not the product of rational deliberation, but, instead, are the result of irrationality, emotion, ritualism, and conformity to reference group pressures (more about this later). While nothing requires that public opinions be informed, and the American public holds uninformed opinions about many important issues, evidence shows that death penalty support is attenuated when subjects are informed about the subject (cf. Bohm & Aveni, 1985; Sarat & Vidmar, 1976; Vidmar & Dittenhoffer, 1981).

Second, because of the hiatus on capital punishment in the United States between 1968 and 1977, the Gallup and other polls conducted during that period (e.g., Ellsworth & Ross, 1983; Sarat & Vidmar, 1976; Thomas & Foster, 1975), are afflicted with the compounded problem of relying on generally uninformed subjects during a time when executions were only an abstract threat. Although there was a flurry of activity following the *Furman* decision in 1972, as 35 states moved quickly to adopt new death penalty statutes, no one was executed during the decade before 1977. As noted below, public opinion about the death penalty is sometimes dramatically different when people consider the death penalty in "concrete" situations (e.g., when people are being executed) rather than in the abstract. Consequently, most of the information available on death penalty opinion, particularly data derived from more recent polls, is based on responses of people who know little about it, and to whom the death penalty is primarily a symbolic issue with essentially no personal or practical relevance (Amsterdam, 1982; Ellsworth & Ross, 1983; Tyler & Weber, 1982).

A third problem is the validity of responses produced from questions about the death penalty in interviews or on questionnaires (see Williams et al., 1988; Harris, 1986; Ellsworth & Ross, 1983). As noted previously, Gallup pollsters (all Gallup poll data on the death penalty have been derived from interviews) have typically asked respondents whether they favored the death penalty for murder or for persons convicted of murder. The questions are ambiguous for at least three reasons. First, they do not distinguish between death penalty opinions for *some* people convicted of murder and for *all* people convicted of murder, including the mentally retarded and juveniles, i.e., youths convicted of murders committed before they turned 18. Second, they do not distinguish between "aggravated" and "nonaggravated" murder. Third, they do not allow for differences in the intensity of support or opposition.

Regarding the first two ambiguities, in the 1976 cases of *Woodson v. North Carolina* (428 U.S. 280) and *Roberts v. Louisiana* (428 U.S. 325) and in the 1987 case of *Sumner v. Shuman* (107 S. Ct. 2716), the Supreme Court rejected mandatory statutes that automatically imposed death sentences for defined capital offenses. In 1977 in the cases of *Coker v. Georgia* (433 U.S. 584) and *Eberheart v. Georgia* (433 U.S. 917), the Supreme Court limited the death penalty almost exclusively to people convicted of "aggravated" murder by banning it for those convicted of the rape of an adult or for kidnapping. Because the American public is not well-informed about the death penalty, and because Gallup pollsters continue to ask people their opinions about mandatory death sentences (the last time was in 1987), most Americans are probably unaware of these restrictions. Nevertheless, recent opinion poll data indicate that the majority of people who favor the death penalty favor it only in certain circumstances, and half of those people who oppose the death penalty are not opposed in an absolute sense (Harris, 1986). Furthermore, the general question cannot reveal the interesting finding that some people who oppose the death penalty do so because they feel the penalty is not severe enough (Bohm, 1989).

As for the issue of whether the death penalty ought to be reserved for "normal" adults, or whether it is appropriate for the mentally retarded or juveniles, the general death penalty question again makes no distinction.[11] The issue is important because in 1987 the U.S. Court of Appeals for the Fifth Circuit affirmed the conviction and death sentence of a 20-year-old mentally retarded man in Texas. The Court of Appeals held that the execution of persons with mental retardation did not violate the Eighth Amendment's prohibition on cruel and unusual punishment. (*Penry v. Lynaugh*, No. 87-6177, review granted at 56 U.S.L.W. 4894)

Regarding juveniles, three people who were juveniles at the time they committed their crimes have been executed in the United States since 1985 and, currently, 31 Americans who were under 18 at the time they committed their crimes are on death rows awaiting execution (*Death Row, U.S.A.*, 1988). According to a recent survey conducted in Georgia, even though a large majority of respondents favor the death penalty in general, 66 percent favor a maximum penalty of life imprisonment for persons convicted of murders committed before they turned 18 (Clearinghouse on Georgia Prisons and Jails, 1987). The issue of the death penalty for children also reveals the often overlooked fact that there is no one death penalty in the United States, but 36 different ones, and some states do not execute children.

Because response categories are generally limited to "favor," "oppose," or "don't know," the typical death penalty question cannot reveal the intensity of support or opposition either. In my own research (Bohm & Aveni, 1985; Bohm, 1989), considerable variation in the intensity of death penalty opinions is found when subjects are asked whether they are "very strongly in favor," "strongly in favor," "somewhat in favor," "undecided," "somewhat opposed," "strongly opposed," or "very strongly oppposed" to several different death penalty conditions. When changes in opinions occur, after participation in a death penalty class, the changed opinions are most likely those of students who initially are "somewhat in favor" of the death penalty or "undecided."

As already noted, for many people who favor capital punishment, support is attenuated when a distinction is made between support in the abstract and support in "concrete" situations (Bohm & Aveni, 1985; Ellsworth & Ross, 1983; Jurow, 1971; Williams et al., 1988). For example, when asked, "If you served on a jury in a trial where the defendant, if found guilty, would automatically be sentenced to death, could you convict that defendant?" several researchers have found that the percentage of respondents who favor the death penalty on the abstract question is substantially reduced when asked about the "concrete" situation (Bohm & Aveni, 1985; Ellsworth & Ross, 1983; Jurow, 1971). Bohm and Aveni (1985) found that, although a majority of subjects favor the death penalty when asked the abstract question ("Do you favor the death penalty for persons convicted of first-degree murder?"), less than a majority of subjects favor it, if they have to take an active part in its administration (i.e., convict in a capital trial or pull the lever that would actuate an execution).

The distinction between "abstract" questions and questions involving "concrete" situations, though important, is somewhat artificial and raises another problem. What people say they will do and what they actually do are often very different (Wicker, 1969). (This explanation may account for the anomaly about the South described earlier.) Research indicates that the largest correlations between people's opinions and their behavior are typically found when the researcher focuses on a specific opinion toward a well-defined situation, which, as noted, is typically not the case in death penalty opinion research. When the opinion is a very general one that is presumed to influence a variety of different situations, as is the case in most death penalty opinion research, much less consistency between opinion and behavior is found (Crespi, 1971). Thus, what people say about the death penalty in general, and what they would do as jurors in a capital murder trial, for example, might very well be different.

CONCLUSION

The aforementioned are only some of the problems with our understanding of American death penalty opinion. They illustrate how little is known about what the American public really thinks of capital punishment, and how superficial and perhaps erroneous that presumed understanding is. They also point to the need for improved research strategies. The Gallup organization began to address some of the problems by asking more questions in the 1986 survey. Recent Media General-Associated Press polls have done likewise (see Harris, 1986). Still, many more questions are begging for answers.

The following are some of the questions that need to be addressed, or addressed more fully, in future research:

1. Why have whites, wealthier people, males, Republicans, and Westerners tended to support the death penalty more than blacks, poorer people, females, Democrats, and Southerners?

2. Why, despite some substantial variation between the attributes of demographic characteristics over both the long- and short-term, have increases and decreases in support and opposition for the attributes of all ten demographic characteristics considered in this chapter followed the aggregate trend?

3. What social events account for variations in the aggregate trend and in specific demographic characteristics over time?

4. Why has the South, compared to the other regions of the United States, voiced the least support for the death penalty, at the same time it has led the nation in executions?

5. How great would support or opposition be if the American public were well-informed about the death penalty and its effects? Some evidence suggests that a majority of Americans would no longer support the death penalty if they were better informed (Sarat & Vidmar, 1976; Vidmar & Dittenhoffer, 1981), while other evidence indicates that becoming informed attenuates support, but may not produce a majority of Americans opposed to the death penalty (Bohm & Aveni, 1985; Bohm, 1989).

6. What do expressions of support and opposition of the death penalty actually mean? Recall that some people oppose the death penalty because they believe it is not severe enough punishment.

7. Would a majority of Americans support the death penalty if they had to actively participate in its administration?

8. What specific conditions are supported or opposed? For example, does a majority of the American public support the death penalty for juveniles or the mentally retarded who commit capital murder?

NOTES

AUTHOR'S NOTE: Thanks to Mike Radelet, John Smykla, Hal Pepinsky, and Les Hill for their helpful comments on an earlier draft of this chapter. Thanks also to Marc Maynard of The Roper Center. Funds for this project were provided by a Faculty Research Grant from Jacksonville State University.

[1] Besides the American Institute of Public Opinion (Gallup), some of the other organizations that have conducted national death penalty opinion surveys are The Roper Organization, the Survey Research Service, National Opinion Research Center, Louis Harris and Associates, the Survey Research Center, Institute for Social Research, and Media General-Associated Press (Harris, 1986; Smith, 1975:310 fn. b).

[2] The three polls excluded from the analysis asked about a mandatory death penalty for anyone convicted of murder and, thus, differed from the more general question asked in the other polls. Interviews for the three excluded polls

were conducted between September 12 and 15, 1980, June 22 and July 13, 1985, and April 25 and May 10, 1987. Also, by using the original data bases stored at The Roper Center for Public Opinion Research in Storrs, CT, several significant errors in the summaries provided by the Gallup Organization are avoided. (The Gallup Organization no longer has its original data bases, as they are stored at The Roper Center.) Percentages reported for the 1957 poll are the most egregious errors in the Gallup summaries. The Gallup summary (Gallup, 1972:1518) shows that in 1957, 47 percent of respondents favored the death penalty, 50 percent opposed it, and 3 percent had no opinion. According to the original data base for 1957, however, 47 percent were in favor, 34 percent were opposed, and 18 percent had no opinion. Instead of 1957 being the year with the highest recorded percentage of opposition to the death penalty, as indicated in the Gallup summary material, information from the original data base reveals that 1957 is notable for the highest percentage of "no opinions" (see Table 8.1).

3   In 1977, in the cases of *Coker v. Georgia* (433 U.S. 584) and *Eberheart v. Georgia* (433 U.S. 917), the Supreme Court generally limited the death penalty to persons convicted of "aggravated" murder by banning it for those convicted of the rape of an adult or kidnapping.

4   Data from all Gallup polls on the death penalty were obtained through interviews with adults. In the 1936 poll, 2,201 adults were interviewed. Samples sizes ranged from 1,008 (November, 1985) to 3,519 (1966).

5   A Gallup poll released in December, 1988, showed that 79 percent of Americans favored the death penalty for murder—the highest level recorded since the first poll in 1936 (Gallup & Gallup, 1988).

6   A 1986 Media General-Associated Press poll revealed that 86 percent of Americans supported the death penalty, 11 percent were opposed, and 3 percent had no opinion. Essentially the same percentage distributions in the 1986 poll were found in the Media General-Associated Press poll conducted two years earlier (*Atlanta Constitution*, 1987). Some local and regional polls have found even greater support for the death penalty. For example, an August, 1987, telephone poll conducted for the *Desert News* of Salt Lake City, Utah, showed that 91 percent of the respondents favored the death penalty for convicted killer Pierre Dale Selby. Selby, 34, and a codefendant, received the death penalty on April 22, 1974, for the murders of three people and the maiming of two others. Testimony indicated that the murderers tortured their victims for four hours, forcing them to drink Drano, and kicking a pen into a victim's ear. The case also was unusual because Selby and his partner are black in a state where less than 1 percent of residents are black and the victims were white. The occasion for the poll was Selby's plea for commutation of his execution. (White, 1987) Significant variation in the percentages reported in different polls during the same year are common.

7   Erskine (1970:295) cites a Harris Survey released on July 3, 1966, that showed that only 38 percent of respondents favored the death penalty, 47 percent were against, and 15 percent had no opinion.

8   Response categories for income or SES vary greatly in the 19 polls. For example, in the 1936 poll, categories are "Avg+," "Avg," "P/P+," and "On relief." Later polls use "Upper," "Middle," and "Lower." In the 1966 poll, categories are

"$7,000 and over," "$5,000-$6,999," "$3,000-$4,999," and "Under $3,000." In the 1967 poll, the upper range was increased to "$15,000 and over" and six categories were used, but in the 1969 poll, the same categories employed in the 1966 poll were repeated. The 1971 poll returned to the six categories in the 1967 poll. In the 1974 poll, five categories were used. The upper limit was "$20,000 and over," while the lower limit was increased to "Under $5,000." In the 1976 poll, the upper limit of "$20,000 and over" was retained, but seven categories were used with the lower limit reduced to "Under $3,000." In the 1981 poll, the upper limit was raised to "$25,000 and over" and six categories were utilized. In the January, 1985 poll, both the upper and lower limits were raised again to "$40,000 and over" and "Under $10,000," respectively. By the November, 1985 poll, the upper limit was again raised to "$50,000 and over." The lower limit of "Under $10,000" was retained. The different response categories used in the different polls make comparisons difficult. For purposes of this study, comparisons were made between the "Top Category" and the "Bottom Category" from each poll. Also, when an odd number of categories were available, the "Middle Category" was used for comparative purposes.

9   For 12 of the 20 polls, the category, "under 30," refers to respondents 18-29 years of age. In the 1971 poll, "under 30" refers to respondents 21-29 years of age. The additional category of 18-20 years of age in that poll was not used. It is noteworthy, however, that in the 1971 poll, respondents 18-20 were substantially less likely to support the death penalty (40%) and more likely to oppose it (54%) than were respondents in the 21-29 group (48 and 43%). In the November, 1972, 1976, 1981, 1982, January, 1985, November, 1985, and 1986 polls, "under 30" refers to respondents 25-29 years of age. The additional category of 18-24 years of age in those polls was not used. Note again that in four of those seven polls (November, 1972, 1976, 1982, and January, 1985) respondents 18-24 were less likely to support and more likely to oppose the death penalty than their 25- to 29-year-old counterparts. However, in the other three polls (1981, November, 1985, and 1986) the opposite was true. Respondents 18-24 were more likely to support and less likely to oppose the death penalty than their 25- to 29-year-old counterparts.

10   In the 1971 poll, 54 percent of respondents in the 18-20 age group also opposed the death penalty (see fn. 9).

11   In the 1986 case of *Ford v. Wainwright* (91 L.Ed. 335), the Supreme Court barred states from executing people who have literally gone crazy on death row.

REFERENCES

Amsterdam, A.G. (1982). "Capital Punishment." In H.A. Bedau (ed.) *The Death Penalty in America, Third Edition,* pp. 346-358. New York: Oxford University Press.

Bedau, H.A. (ed.) (1982). *The Death Penalty in America, Third Edition.* New York: Oxford University Press.

Bohm, R.M. (1989). "The Effects of Classroom Instruction and Discussion on Death Penalty Opinions: A Teaching Note." *Journal of Criminal Justice,* 17:123-131.

_____ (1987). "American Death Penalty Attitudes: A Critical Examination of Recent Evidence." *Criminal Justice and Behavior,* 14:380-396.

Bohm, R.M. & A.F. Aveni (1985). "Knowledge and Attitude about the Death Penalty: A Test of the Marshall Hypotheses." Paper presented at the annual meeting of the American Society of Criminology, November, 1985, San Diego, CA.

Bowers, W.J. with G.L. Pierce & J.F. McDevitt (1984). *Legal Homicide: Death As Punishment in America, 1864-1982.* Boston: Northeastern University Press.

Clearinghouse on Georgia Prisons and Jails (1987). "Juveniles and the Death Penalty: Poll Documents Voters' Opinions." Clearinghouse on Georgia Prisons and Jails: Atlanta, GA 30301.

Combs, M.W. & J.C. Comer (1982). "Race and Capital Punishment: A Longitudinal Analysis." *Phylon,* 43:350-359.

Crespi, I. (1971). "What Kinds of Attitude Measures Are Predictive of Behavior?" *Public Opinion Quarterly,* 35:327-334.

Death Row, U.S.A. (1988). New York: NAACP Legal Defense and Educational Fund, Inc. (August 1).

Ellsworth, P.C. & L. Ross (1983). "Public Opinion and Capital Punishment: A Close Examination of the Views of Abolitionists and Retentionists." *Crime and Delinquency,* 29:116-169.

Erikson, R.S. (1976). "The Relationship between Public Opinion and State Policy: A New Look at Some Forgotten Data." *American Journal of Political Science,* 20:25-36.

Erskine, H. (1970). "The Polls: Capital Punishment." *Public Opinion Quarterly,* 34:290-307.

Gallup, G.H. (1987). *The Gallup Poll: Public Opinion 1986.* Wilmington, DE: Scholarly Resources, Inc.

_____ (1972). *The Gallup Poll: Public Opinion 1935-1971* (Volumes 1-3). New York: Random House.

Gallup, G., Jr. & A. Gallup (1988). "Public Support for Death Penalty is Highest in Gallup Annals." Los Angeles Times Syndicate.

Gelles, R.J. & M.A. Straus (1976). "Family Experience and Public Support of the Death Penalty." In H.A. Bedau & C.M. Pierce (eds.) *Capital Punishment in the United States*, pp. 227-246. New York: AMS Press.

Harris, P. (1986). "Oversimplification and Error in Public Opinion Surveys on Capital Punishment." *Justice Quarterly*, 3:429-455.

Jurow, G.L. (1971). "New Data on the Effect of a 'Death Qualified' Jury on the Guilt Determination Process." *Harvard Law Review*, 84:567-611.

Monroe, A.D. (1979). "Consistency between Public Preferences and National Policy Decisions." *American Politics Quarterly*, 7:3-19.

Oskamp, S. (1977). *Attitudes and Opinions*. Englewood Cliffs, NJ: Prentice-Hall.

Page, B.I. & R.Y. Shapiro (1983). "Effects of Public Opinion on Policy." *American Political Science Review*, 77:175-190.

Page, B.I., R.Y. Shapiro & G.R. Dempsey (1987). "What Moves Public Opinion?" *American Political Science Review*, 81:23-43.

Perkes, A.C. and R. Schildt (1979). "Death-Related Attitudes of Adolescent Males and Females." *Death Education*, 2:359-368.

Rusche, G. & O. Kirchheimer (1968). *Punishment and Social Structure*. New York: Russell and Russell.

Sarat, A. & N. Vidmar (1976). "Public Opinion, The Death Penalty, and the Eighth Amendment: Testing the Marshall Hypothesis." *Wisconsin Law Review*, 17:171-206.

Smith, T.W. (1975). "A Trend Analysis of Attitudes Toward Capital Punishment, 1936-1974." In J.E. Davis (ed.) *Studies of Social Change Since 1948, Volume II*, pp. 257-318. University of Chicago: National Opinion Research Center.

Thomas, C.W. & S.C. Foster (1975). "A Sociological Perspective on Public Support for Capital Punishment." *American Journal of Orthopsychiatry*, 45:641-657.

Tyler, T.R. & R. Weber (1982). "Support For The Death Penalty: Instrumental Response To Crime, Or Symbolic Attitude?" *Law and Society Review*, 17:21-45.

Vidmar, N. & T. Dittenhoffer (1981). "Informed Public Opinion and Death Penalty Attitudes." *Canadian Journal of Criminology*, 23:43-56.

Vidmar, N. & P. Ellsworth (1974). "Public Opinion and the Death Penalty." *Stanford Law Review*, 26:1245-1270.

Vidmar, N. & D.T. Miller (1980). "Social Psychological Processes Underlying Attitudes Toward Legal Punishment." *Law and Society Review*, 14:565-602.

Weissberg, R. (1976). *Public Opinion and Popular Government*. Englewood Cliffs, NJ: Prentice-Hall.

White, M. (1987). "Indignation Over Torture Killings Spurs Death Drive." *Anniston (Alabama) Star,* August 17.

Wicker, A.W. (1969). "Attitudes Versus Actions: The Relationship of Verbal and Overt Behavioral Responses to Attitude Objects." *Journal of Social Issues,* 25:41-78.

Williams, F.P., D.R. Longmire & D.B. Gulick (1988). "The Public and the Death Penalty: Opinion as an Artifact of Question Type." *Criminal Justice Research Bulletin,* 3:1-5.

Zimring, F.E. & G. Hawkins (1986). *Capital Punishment and the American Agenda.* Cambridge: Cambridge University Press.

About the Authors

William C. Bailey is Professor of Sociology and Associate Dean of the Graduate School at Cleveland State University. He received his doctoral degree in Sociology from Washington State University in 1971. His major research interests include crime and deterrence, capital punishment, and urban crime patterns.

Robert M. Bohm is Associate Professor in the Department of Criminal Justice at the University of North Carolina at Charlotte. He received his Ph.D. in Criminology from Florida State University in 1980. His research interests are diverse, but recently he has been focusing on the issue of capital punishment in the United States, especially death penalty opinion.

Thomas J. Keil is Chair and Professor of Sociology at the University of Louisville. His most recent work, *On Strike! Capital Cities and the Wilkes-Barre Newspaper Unions,* was published by the University of Alabama Press.

Pat Koester is the former Executive Director of the National Clearinghouse on Jails and Prisons.

Edward J. Latessa is Professor and Chair of the Department of Criminal Justice at the University of Cincinnati. He has published in the area of corrections; most recently on intensive supervision of probationers and parolees and prison technology. He also is Past President of the Academy of Criminal Justice Sciences.

Marilyn D. McShane received her Ph.D. in Criminal Justice from Sam Houston State University in 1985. She has worked in corrections as a prerelease counselor, a paralegal for inmate assistance, and as Director of a statewide corrections program in Texas. Currently, she is Associate Professor in the Department of Criminal Justice at California State University, San Bernardino. She is co-author, with Frank Williams, of the text *Criminological Theory.*

Raymond Paternoster is Associate Professor in the Institute of Criminal Justice and Criminology at the University of Maryland. His current research interests include testing an expanded notion of the deterrence doctrine and determining the operative factors employed by jurors in imposing the life or death sentence.

Victoria Schneider is Archival Assistant Director at the Inter-University Consortium for Political and Social Research (ICPSR) at the University of Michigan. She also is principal investigator and project manager of the National Archive of Criminal Justice Data sponsored by the Bureau of Justice Statistics, U.S. Department of Justice. Her interests range from studies of victimization such as the National Crime Surveys to work on capital punishment, youth corrections, and issues of secondary data analysis.

John O. Smykla is Professor and Chair of the Department of Criminal Justice at the University of Alabama. At present he is doing historical criminology on capital punishment and the impact of Reconstruction on southern law enforcement. He also does research on comparative criminal justice, especially in Latin America.

Gennaro F. Vito is Professor in the School of Justice Administration at the University of Louisville. He is presently at work on a study of capital sentencing in Kentucky, a death penalty survey, crime pattern analysis and drug testing of probationers and parolees. He is editor of *The American Journal of Criminal Justice*.

Frank P. Williams III is Professor and Chair of the Department of Criminal Justice at California State University, San Bernardino. He received his Ph.D. in Criminology from Florida State University in 1976. The author of many publications and governmental reports, including *Criminological Theory* with Prentice-Hall, he has research interests in several criminological areas, among them capital punishment, corrections, and drug abuse issues.

Deborah G. Wilson is Policy Advisor, Kentucky Office of the Attorney General, Director of the Kentucky Criminal Justice Statistical Analysis Center, and Associate Professor, School of Justice Administration at the University of Louisville. She has published studies on long-term inmates, elderly inmates, intensive supervision of probationers and parolees, and prison population projections.